P9-DDJ-323

FOUR WORTHIES

By the same author

ENGLISH FOLK

THE SCOT IN HISTORY

FOUR WORTHIES

John Chamberlain, Anne Clifford,
John Taylor, Oliver Heywood

by

WALLACE NOTESTEIN

NEW HAVEN
YALE UNIVERSITY PRESS
1957

PRINTED IN GREAT BRITAIN

CONTENTS

ILLUSTRATIONS

ACKNOWLEDGMENTS

FOR permission to quote from *The Diary of Lady Anne Clifford* (Heinemann, London, 1923) I am grateful to the editor, the Hon. V. Sackville-West. To the firm of Titus Wilson & Son, Kendal, Westmorland, I owe permission to use excerpts from manuscripts quoted by Dr. George C. Williamson in his massive work, *Lady Anne Clifford, Countess of Dorset, Pembroke and Montgomery, 1590-1666, Her Life, Letters and Work* (1922). President Norman Egbert McClure of Ursinus College, Collegeville, Pennsylvania, has graciously allowed me the right to quote from his edition, *The Letters of John Chamberlain* (Philadelphia, 1939). He was also good enough to read my essay on Chamberlain and to make a correction in a date.

For the right to use the pictures shown in this book I must thank several people. Unfortunately there is no known portrait of John Chamberlain. But it is possible to offer presentments of his closest friend, Sir Dudley Carleton. For his portrait I wish to thank the Trustees of the National Portrait Gallery. To that institution I owe also the portrait of Anne, Lady Clifford, as an old lady. The Bodleian Library at Oxford was good enough to furnish me with a copy of the portrait in their possession of John Taylor.

In particular I wish to thank Mr. David T. Piper of the National Portrait Gallery, who has taken a great deal of pains to help me in the matter of the pictures.

W. N.

INTRODUCTION

THE four characters chosen for portraiture in this book have long interested the writer as individuals who have much to tell of the times in which they lived. Each of them is worth elaborate examination as a person, and such examination is made possible by the body of sources available. We are able to learn something of their attitudes towards their fellows and of what their fellows thought of them. If we can in some degree put ourselves into the minds and feelings of even a few men and women we shall understand more of that time, see a little further into a scene at best but dimly lighted. Not that we shall ever understand it as well as we would. We keep gazing from afar, from three hundred years away, at those figures, who seem always to recede slowly from our view. We hope that we may come up close to them and look upon them full-face, as we would upon our friends today. But they slip off into the shadow, for ever elusive. We are well aware that our books and manuscripts are not enough, that they reveal only small segments of the truth, but they are all we have.

The four characters selected for study are not more typical of their people and time than many others. To call any particular individuals typical of their nation and century is hazardous. What can be said is that each of the four was thoroughly English.

A woman like Anne, Lady Clifford, is inconceivable in any but an English setting. No countess in a Bavarian hill-topping castle or in a château along the Loire would have stood up to her sovereign and have resisted the pressures of a time-serving Court as did the Countess of Dorset. She exhibited moreover an outspokenness characteristic of the English countryside then and now. Her frankness and directness were only exceeded by her kindness, and that was English too. She could tell off those who had hurt her and as quickly forgive them.

John Chamberlain was not quite as plain-spoken – he was not country-born – but he had an engaging English frankness, at least with his intimates. Something else he had that was English; a way of explaining a situation with a considered moderation. Moderation was, I think, natural to him, but it had been inbred in the English of that time from their reading of Roman writers.

John Taylor was far removed in background and breeding from Anne, Lady Clifford, and from John Chamberlain. He was a waterman turned poetaster in order to better his lot. Like many an ingenious Englishman of the time he landed on his feet and did well by himself. He was an assertive, aggressive John Bull, almost a 'thruster' in the language of today. But wherever he happened to be, men gathered round him to listen and others pressed hospitality upon him. If he had been a shade more middle-class he might have qualified as one of Matthew Arnold's Philistines, somewhat pre-Victorian. He was too much a common man to be called vulgar.

Oliver Heywood may seem less distinctively English than the other three characters. He was not like the English of song and story, nor out of merry England, but he belonged nevertheless in the thorough-going Puritan tradition, and nothing was more purely English. He would have been at home with John Bunyan and Richard Baxter and with the Nonconformist leaders of the eighteenth and nineteenth centuries. He had something in common with the great Scottish ministers but with an English difference.

Our four characters were of course somewhat like the English of today and yet, I suspect, as removed from them as are the Americans of our own decades. They belonged in their century and it behoves us to regard them not only as individuals but as creatures of their day. It is well for us to recall some of the characteristics of the English of that time that may seem relevant to our four.

One gains an impression from Chamberlain's letters that the men with whom he consorted in Paul's Walk and on country terraces were an out-going and on-coming people. The inhabitants of the north country whom Oliver Heywood knew were less tamed and sophisticated but, with some marked exceptions, they were also a friendly folk. The innkeepers, mayors and country gentlemen who showed favour to the itinerant John Taylor were good fellows, nearly all of them. The Westmorland cottagers whom the Dowager Countess of Dorset and Pembroke encountered on her rough journeys over the mountains were, we may be allowed to guess, not much in awe of the great lady. No matter how much she valued her high state she knew how to make friends with moorland farmers. The evidence we find of the affability of the English from the records of our four characters can be many times matched. Nicander Nucius in 1545 declared of the English:

> Their nobles and rulers and those in authority are replete with benevolence, and courteous to strangers.

A physician writing about his visits to England in 1560 said:

> They be people very civil and well-affected to men well stricken in years, and to such as bear any countenance and estimation of learning . . . Frankly to utter what I think of the incredible courtesy and friendliness used in this famous realm I must needs confess it doth surmount and carry away the prize of all others.

The Venetian ambassadors to England in their reports home were wont to emphasize the friendliness of the English, but not always. One of them reported that the English were hostile to foreigners and not very friendly among themselves.

The affability and friendliness of the English were by no means characteristic of all of them. Up and down the country, in north Hertfordshire, on the western slopes of the Cotswolds, on the lower Severn and far up the Severn, and in many other districts dwelt men who were anything but cordial to strangers and who were a worry to the parson and a tribulation to the justices of the peace. A Spanish ambassador in England remarked that the flour (meaning the gentry) was very choice, but that the bran (meaning the common people) was very coarse. The statement would need modification, for many common people were of a sturdy law-abiding stock. But it is true that the rural parts were here and there given up to men almost savage. The reader of the chapter on Oliver Heywood will come upon some of the wild moormen of the West Riding.

A good-natured people, the English were called by a Swiss traveller in the late seventeenth century. The adjective means more than affable and one might question its applicability to the people of the late sixteenth and early seventeenth centuries. But they were something else, or some of them were, a generous people and at times more than generous, concerned with the welfare of the community.

The generosity of the gentry and of the nobility was more than mere *noblesse oblige*. Anne, Lady Clifford, Dowager Countess of Dorset and Pembroke, poured out her beneficence on almost everyone within her range. Oliver Heywood was a Yorkshireman and liked to accumulate shillings but he was kind to all those who came to his door and to many others. It cannot be said that the water-poet was generous but he was the recipient of a great deal of generosity.

Those representatives of the best of the gentry, the justices of the peace, were sometimes extremely generous. In seasons of scarcity and high prices they would dip into their own pockets to buy wheat for the poor; they would come to the rescue of those ruined by fire and flood. Other gentlemen allowed their tenants, when hard-pressed, to have time to pay their rents, and raised those rents only when prodded into doing so by family lawyers. The complaints of the time against grasping landlords prove how accustomed was the countryside to landlords who were considerate and kindly.

Next to personal generosity was a certain generosity of outlook. John Chamberlain had something of it. He was a critical old bachelor who saw through shams and disliked pride and pomp, but he could grow indignant over the drafting of poor men for military service abroad, and he resented religious persecution.

The men who set up the Elizabethan Welfare State, who put through at length the Poor Laws of 1597 and of 1601, were public-spirited, or as we would say, liberal-minded. Just who were really responsible for that beneficent legislation, whether Privy Councillors or Members of Parliament, we do not know, but they did something notable in English history, they provided methods of helping the needy and helpless that were to be used until the nineteenth century. It hardly detracts from their credit that those famous pieces of legislation were the final outcome of law-making for the poor over a long period. We need not lessen the praise for them because they were no doubt partly concerned to prevent disorder that might blaze into rebellion. It is often said and with some justice that there was not much pity in the Elizabethan world but the Poor Laws prove that some did exist. It may be suspected – it has indeed been suspected – that the Puritan leaders of the House of Commons had a part in pushing through those excellent Acts. In any case the passage of such legislation indicated a generous attitude upon the part of the English. We think of the English today as among the most liberal-minded of peoples, with a great willingness to help the distressed, and we are not surprised to discover anticipations of that pleasant trait three centuries and more ago.

A conventional zeal for morality can be detected in the writings of John Taylor. Like Calvin Coolidge's preacher he was against sin. Drinking, swearing, wenching he denounced with tiresome and gleeful iteration, knowing that his audience would be with him. Oliver Heywood, as a good Presbyterian, was of course a moralist and was constantly horrified at the drunkenness and incontinence of the hill people, horrified and interested. John Chamberlain was a refreshingly different person, never surprised at the frailties of humankind, but distressed at the open infractions of accepted codes. As for the Countess of Dorset, she had a long young-womanhood at the Court among great ladies whose sins were as scarlet and she was remarkably reticent about them. But she derived her ideas as to right and wrong from the Old Testament, where sin was sin and was soon punished. Our four characters were all of them old English in their traditions, and the old English were moralistic. One cannot read Langland, Gower and Skelton without catching the indignation of those writers about the abuses and wickedness of the time. Chaucer, too, was aware that all was not well. The records of the boroughs show that the rulers of those bodies shared the outlook of the writers. They made many regulations to uphold decency and to punish those who did not conform. The English towns and the countryside, but particularly the towns, were intent upon proper behaviour in their communities long before they were touched by Puritanism. It is true that not all the countryside lived up to the ideals of the time. In the deep country, in remote villages off the main roads, where public opinion had little sway, were to be found whole families and groups of families run down at the heels. The countryside needed here and there the moral yearnings of the middle classes in towns.

What saddened John Chamberlain more than wickedness in high places and wenching in low was the general corruption of the times. He was so accustomed to it that he had little to say about it but he realized that there was much wrong in his country. The men at the head of affairs were pocketing huge sums for themselves and their subordinates were imitating them. The business world was no better; the managers of companies and their underlings and the factors at the various ports were enriching themselves at the expense of their organizations. Chamberlain may not have known of another abuse, the bribing of juries, which was carried on all over the realm. Smyth of Nibley complained of the wholesale way in which juries were bought and probably himself became an adept in the hidden art.

The fluidity of society appears throughout the letters of John Chamberlain; appears indeed in almost every letter. New knights by the score, new baronets, new barons, new earls and then a new duke, the promotions came thick and fast and men could see that the way to honours and titles was to woo favourites. The Court watched the great game played before them and tried to spot the winners and losers, and no one was more interested than John Chamberlain. In Heywood's diaries another game was to be seen, the struggle in the North for business success. Men were starting new enterprises, making fortunes or going to the wall. All over England men were climbing recklessly from one rung of the ladder to another and now and then falling off.

The men who forced their way up by initiative and energy were many, but more numerous, at least in urban circles, were those who did not expect to get ahead by hard work and talent. The way to fly high was to get under the wing of someone and mount with him or be pushed up by him. To be sure, men did win to position by sheer merit, as Smyth of Nibley, Lionel Cranfield, Ralph Winwood, Thomas Edmondes, Dudley Carleton, John Williams and others. Merit counted most, I think, in the Civil Service and least possibly in the Church. But merit had a bad time getting started. Most of those who arrived at some dignity or honourable post had in the beginning gained the interest of a nobleman or of a minister of state, or of a bishop, or had friends at the university or in one of the Inns of Court. Not a few young men established themselves by means of a marriage into an influential family. In the business world were countless men who had got on by marrying the widow or daughter of the owner of the business.

It was a time when good men who refused to play up to royal favourites found themselves out of luck. Such men as George Herbert, William Hakewill, John Preston and John Donne failed to go as far as their talents should have carried them. John Chamberlain himself was a person who might have done well if he had entered the race for power. Below the men in that race were thousands of men who had no expectation of any considerable success but aspired only to posts with a modest income where the work was not heavy and could be largely done by subordinates.

Our four characters may have seldom heard the phrase 'common sense', but already some of the English looked at things from a common-sense point of view. The reader of Chamberlain's letters comes to realize that both Chamberlain and his friend, Rowland Lytton, were given to a certain down-to-earth attitude. Chamberlain was likely to suspect the non-English of not having common sense, of being queer and even fantastic, especially the Scots and the Welsh. Shakespeare would have agreed with Chamberlain about that matter. He presented Hotspur as regarding the Welsh as a strange people. He makes Hotspur say of Glendower:

> Sometimes he angers me
> With telling me of the mouldwarp and the ant,
> Of the dreamer Merlin, and his prophecies,
> And of a dragon and a finless fish,

> A clip-wing'd griffin and a moulten raven,
> A crouching lion and a rampant cat,
> And such a deal of skimble-skamble stuff
> As puts me in a faint.

In other words Hotspur was an Englishman and did not care for 'skimble-skamble stuff'. The English were not dreamers taken in by tales of Merlin, but hard-headed men who tolerated no nonsense. Hotspur's wife pooh-poohed sentimentality. John Chamberlain had much the same attitude. He smiled at the fond ways of James I. He recognized the claims of friendship and would go to a great deal of trouble for Carleton and Winwood but he made no fuss over them and told them just what he thought, as became a proper Englishman.

Three of our four characters moved in an easy-going milieu. John Chamberlain seemed, like many Englishmen, less busy than he was; he had no fixed occupation and occupied himself in serving his friends. The possession of a landed income enabled many of those friends to fleet the time carelessly as they did in the golden world. Anne, Lady Clifford, was born to the purple and neither she nor her friends knew anything about making a living. John Taylor found himself an occupation that did not hold him close to a routine and allowed him time to talk on the streets. Oliver Heywood was the only busy man among our four characters and much of his time was spent upon his knees. No doubt a majority of Englishmen were more occupied than our four friends, but a large number of them were not inclined to overdo it. Van Meteren, a Dutch merchant and traveller, observed that the English were not as industrious as the Netherlanders or the French. Venetian ambassadors at the English Court in their letters home said as much of the English. One of them in 1620 wrote that the English had an excessive inclination to comfort and pleasure. Mrs. Hutchinson spoke of the plenty of the country and remarked that the inhabitants, not forced to toil for their bread, 'have ever addicted themselves to more generous [highborn] employments'. We may guess that the tempo of English life at that time was not rapid and that in the country men and women went about their appointed tasks without hustle or bustle. There was a proverb then:

> He that will thrive must rise at five,
> But he that hath thriven may lye till seaven.

No doubt there were many who worked long hours, the shop-keeping class, many of the yeomen, and possibly the farm-labourers. Even those groups may not have striven as earnestly as continental people of like degree. Moreover England was a large, fertile territory where wheat, barley, rye and vetch abounded, where the paled-off woodland was full of deer and the woods on the common land crowded with pigs. Geese and ducks and chickens flourished. There was food enough for everyone if it had been well distributed, and there were few large towns and no proper cities except London. There was still a good deal of timber and there was an increasing supply of coal. In general the English, except for the unfortunate, should not in their demi-Eden have been driven by want to overwork. Even today the Englishman is reluctant to admit that he is a hard worker and prefers to make you believe that he is a lily of the field, the reverse of the American who would fain persuade you over his two hours for lunch that he is a slave to his calling.

It is possible that one of the several reasons for the easy-going Englishman was the example of the country gentleman. The man in the manor house was the king of the village. He and his wife set the standards of manners and of conduct. They had leisure, and the man of the house sometimes devoted that leisure to local government, acting as a justice of the peace, or high constable, or commissioner of this and that. Occasionally he espoused what he called the 'retired life', and gave himself up to meditation and reading, or perhaps to gardening and planting. More often he hunted hares and brought down stags. He was closely observed by his tenants. They could not but crave for themselves some of the leisure enjoyed by their betters. The artisan and the shop-keeper and the wool-merchant laboured long so that their offspring might fare better than they and enjoy the luxury of time to spare. They worked hard but they vaguely realized that working hard was a badge of inferiority in a nation where the gentleman dominated the scene. I cannot remember that anyone in the seventeenth century was ever praised for being hard-working. On the other hand the gentry and the nobility were now and then accused by the Puritan clergy of living idly. It was a charge that revealed what people had been thinking; it was to be made more often when the Civil Wars broke out and the criticism by the middle-class man of the social system, long unspoken, began to be uttered aloud and set down in print. The charge was typical of the Puritans, who believed that next to godliness was zeal in one's occupation. Implicit in Calvinism was the strenuous life.

The resistance to the gospel of the strenuous life is likely to be greatest in a prosperous country such as England had been in the late Elizabethan and early Stuart days. 'Need makes the old wife trot', went the proverb, but, we might add, 'if the cupboard was full the old wife could sit down, at least until she had to start cooking'. A philosophy of history quite as sound as many now offered might be built up around the notion that nemesis follows those nations who grow fat, if we grant that nemesis is leaden-footed.

It has to be said that some of the gentle classes were by no means given over to pleasant inactivity. It was whispered in Kent that the Colpeppers could not lie still in their graves, and the same might have been whispered of restless driving families in other counties. Younger sons abounded in the England of James I and they were forced to be more active than their fathers; they became factors in companies, they opened or developed mines, they sent ships to sea. To learn of the adventurous and imaginative Englishmen one may well turn to the pages of the Hakluyt Society and follow the stories of explorers who sought the Northwest and the Northeast Passages, who pushed their way through the White Sea to Russia and down through Russia to the Caspian Sea and Persia. Other Englishmen made competition for the Venetians and the French in the Mediterranean; still others found their way to India and established trading posts and took the gorgeous East in fee.

The reader may have read between the lines that the English were not wholly unaware of their own worth. National self-esteem is not uncommon. The superiority of the English is implicit in the letters of Chamberlain and more than implicit in the doggerel of the water-poet. To brag of his country increased Taylor's good opinion of himself. The literature of the time is full of the glories of the island people. Were they not better and braver fighters than their foes? Was it not on record that one man from Devonshire could drive eight Dons up a narrow street? Was it not understood that in a world of deceitful men, Dutch and French and Italian, the English were men of their word? The continentals who visited the island smiled at the complacency of the inhabitants. It was an old jest among them that when an Englishman wished to praise you he told you that you could easily be mistaken for an Englishman.

The predisposition of the English in favour of their own people was reinforced by their pride in the past of those people. Said Mrs. Hutchinson:

> Whoever considers the English will find it no small favour of God to have been one of its natives . . . The celebrated glory

> of this Isle's inhabitants confers some honour upon every one of her children.

Few English there were who would not have agreed with her. We all recall a famous passage in Milton:

> Why else was this Nation chosen before any other that out of her as out of Zion, should be proclaimed and sounded forth the first tidings and trumpet of the Reformation . . . Now once again God is decreeing to begin some new and great period in the Church . . . what does He then but reveal Himself to His servants, and, as His manner is, first to His Englishman.

The playwrights and the scribblers would not have put it just like that but they would have believed that when things needed to be done, the Englishman was the man to do it. In some degree it was that faith that made the British Empire and kept it going.

The English had some right to feel superior. When Ralph Sadleir served as Elizabeth's Ambassador to Scotland he remarked that the Scots lacked men of 'wit, gravity, learning, or experience . . . to take a hand in the direction of things'. Such men the English had in plenty and more than most peoples. The middle classes, who furnish most of the talent at all times, were increasing in numbers and influence. The yeomen, the burgesses in country towns and in London, the professional classes, and the gentry, especially the smaller gentry, were turning out by the hundreds young men with active, sharp and reflective minds. Many of them were being given a rigorous training at the universities and at the Inns of Court, many more relatively than ever before. During the Tudor rule such young men were beginning to get or make their chance. Queen Elizabeth had an eye always open to find ability and, when she found it, put it to work and gave it scope. Young men of promise in many fields were moving on London. When there was a wide distribution of talent and when much of that talent was gathered into one great centre it followed that the best would be good indeed, serviceable to the state 'in the direction of things', and serviceable in all the professions and arts. The confluence of ability in one place and its effects required time to make themselves evident. 'An able man', wrote Smyth of Nibley, 'is long in breeding', and a galaxy of able men is longer in breeding. That galaxy made its appearance towards the close of the Queen's reign but shone during the next half-century. In politics and parliament, in the Civil Service and diplomacy, in the Church, in the law, in prose and poetry, in the drama, there were altogether scores of men of eminence; above them at the top were more than a dozen figures whose claims to greatness could not be denied, and at least five of lasting significance.

JOHN CHAMBERLAIN

JOHN CHAMBERLAIN

I

WHAT are we to make of anyone who lived before 1700, writes a recent essayist in *The Times Literary Supplement*, meaning that we cannot hope to understand those who lived earlier. One might mention Pepys, who, a generation before 1700, offered many clues as to his inmost being and some as to the men and women around him. But if we go further back we find it progressively harder to know enough about any personality to interpret him adequately. How much more difficult is it to catch the thoughts and feelings of anyone of an earlier generation? The Paston letters tell us something of a Norfolk family of the fifteenth century but even the leading members of that interesting connection appear in a dim medieval light.

Yet, two generations before Pepys set down in cipher his intimate thoughts, were written the letters of John Chamberlain. They constitute the first considerable body of letters in English history and literature that the modern reader can easily follow and, if he will examine them with attention, can thoroughly enjoy. Those letters reveal to us in no small degree the men and women of the last years of Elizabeth and of the whole reign of James I and they offer us many clues as to the letter-writer himself.

Those letters in print and manuscript have long been available to scholars.[1] Through Norman Egbert McClure's complete edition of them in two large volumes they are now reaching a

[1] They were quoted again and again by historians in the nineteenth century. A century ago the letters covering the last years of Elizabeth's reign were published by the Camden Society and many of the later letters appear in the two volumes gathered by Thomas Birch and later published as *The Court and Times of James I.* S. R. Gardiner, the historian of the Stuart period, depended in no small degree upon the statements made by Chamberlain and so have all other historians of the period.

larger public. That edition will, I hope, sooner or later be reprinted with the spelling modernized and a full index. When that is done the letters will find their way into sets of minor English classics and historians will devote space to John Chamberlain in their historiographical writings and estimate his accuracy with the finest measuring rods. Essayists in *belles-lettres* will discover him with self-satisfaction and hail their find.

He was more skilled than most well-known letter-writers in appraising his contemporaries. Like the best novelists he did not present character-sketches of his personae but allowed them to speak and act for themselves. The list of personae was not small. He was part of a circle of gentlefolk living in the country near London and of London Civil Servants, two closely related groups. He knew many other people and those whom he did not know he heard about from friends. In his gallery he exhibited most of the notables of the realm: James I, Robert Cecil, Francis Bacon, Edward Coke, Walter Ralegh, Thomas Bodley, Ralph Winwood, Henry Wotton, Inigo Jones, Ben Jonson, Lancelot Andrewes, John Donne and many others. If he knew about men and their habits and foibles he understood also the spirit of the time. From him we can learn how events impressed an intelligent contemporary. To know Chamberlain in and out, his comings and goings, his reports of what occurred and what was said, is to come close to living in his generation.

It was his business and pleasure to record events, usually small events. A large majority of his letters were addressed to his young friend, Dudley Carleton, who, when he became a diplomat on the Continent, needed to know the latest from London. Chamberlain constituted himself a news-gatherer for his friend, an unprofessional one.[1] A Paul's-walker he called himself, and so he

[1] As far back as 1588 Chamberlain, in a letter to Stephen Powle, suggested further correspondence: 'If you like it, you may have more [letters], for I will not fail to answer you by exchange . . . I love not to take too much pains, nor to wear my wits, and therefore I have sent you this assay.' Tanner MSS. (Bodley), 309, ff. 56-7.

was, one of the group of men who stepped back and forth in St. Paul's talking to people and pumping them for information. From most such walkers he differed in that his information was for a single friend[1] and in that he received no money for his services.

For such men the old St. Paul's furnished opportunities.[2] It was the centre of the City of London, and of the wider London that had grown up outside, and indeed of all England. It was as full of activity as an ant-heap, too much so to please the godly. Hawkers cried their wares in the nave of the Church, beggars swarmed about its walls, and inside and out, as weather changed, went back and forth a procession of men on the look-out.

There were to be heard the latest public occurrents, whether in politics, war, religion, or society, much that could be found in a modern newspaper and a great deal besides, backstairs gossip and rumours of every kind. There were to be seen copies of proclamations, of pamphlets, and of new books. If one would know about the King and his Council, or about the speeches uttered in the House of Commons, he had the chance to find out at Paul's. If one's taste ran to the sermons of John Donne, or to the poems of Sidney, one might come across them either in transcribed written copies or in printed forms. There one could enjoy the

[1] Yet Winwood received a good many letters from Chamberlain. Lancelot Andrewes, when Bishop of Winchester, asked Chamberlain not to forget him when he had any news.

[2] Francis Osborne, recalling his own youth, described the business of Paul's-walking. 'It was the fashion of those times, and did so continue till these . . . for the principal gentry, lords, courtiers, and men of all professions not merely mechanic, to meet in Paul's Church by eleven and walk in the middle aisle till twelve, and after dinner from three to six, during which times some discoursed on business, others of news. Now in regard of the universal commerce there happened little that did not first or last arrive here . . . And those news-mongers, as they called them, did not only take the boldness to weigh the public but most intrinsic actions of the state, which some courtier or other did betray to this society. Amongst whom divers being very rich had great sums owing them by such as stood next the throne, who by this means were rendered in a manner their pensioners. So as I have found since little reason to question the truth of what I heard then, but much to confirm me in it.' *Works* (1689, 9th ed.), pp. 449-51.

John Earle in his *Microcosmographie* called Paul's walk 'the land's epitome . . . the lesser isle of Great Britain . . . the whole world's map . . . nothing liker Babel'.

latest quip whether at its inception or when it attained circulation.

For thirty years Chamberlain watched and listened. Every item of news and of well-supported gossip[1] that he could pick up he passed on by letter to his friend. He had a talent for exact and illuminating detail. 'I am well acquainted', wrote his friend, Powle, in the late 1580s, 'how much particular circumstances do delight you.' It is of course not an historical interpretation that he offers us, but a running, lively narrative of the news as it came out from day to day. Yet he was by no means unaware of the meanings behind words, and he knew how much depended upon an exact order in which a series of events occurred. His quiet explanations of how a matter stood and his estimates of opinion are as useful to the historian today as they were to an aspiring diplomat three hundred years ago.

Of course to one who has had to examine many news-letters, the tricks and conventions of the news-writer appear. Chamberlain's letters are not unlike those written by Thomas Lock, Thomas Lorkin and Joseph Mead. Sometimes Chamberlain writes almost the same letter to Carleton and to Winwood, and one can discover how carefully carved was every sentence.[2] Sometimes there is a phrase which he originated and which he liked and used more than once. When he realized that he had little to tell he put in parenthesis the sentence: 'I love not altogether idle and empty letters', and repeated the sentence three months later. His humour had occasionally something of a formula about it and yet it is lighter than that of most letter-writers of the time, as when he says of the King: 'His speech lasted above an hour although he commended brevity very much.'

[1] Much news, he recognized, was 'only of matches, marriages, christenings, creations, knightings, and such like', which was small beer, and yet he set it down.

[2] I do not believe that he rewrote them, rather that he spent much time in thinking them out and then penned them slowly. Writing was too tedious a process to change and alter. Robert Cecil in his official letters to ambassadors often erased whole sentences and rewrote them between the lines and sent them off in that form.

He referred to the vogue for the daughter-in-law of Cecil and adds that people say: 'Great is Diana of the Cecilians.'[1]

Chamberlain's reports have an incidental importance which he, a self-effacing man, would not have foreseen; they preserve a portrait of a London gentleman. That portrait emerges slowly, for the correspondence is copious and largely impersonal. A creature necessarily of his own day he was nevertheless an English type that might have been found in any recent century, more often in the country than in London. We could not ask for a more representative middle-of-the-road Englishman in the period of transition between the confident days of Elizabeth and the doubting and divided days of the Stuarts than this unobtrusive and agreeable Londoner. His good manners and his quiet reserve were those of the best type of country gentleman; his ability to quote French, Italian and Spanish phrases, his knowledge of the old writers of England and those of Rome reveal him as a cultivated citizen of the world.

Not quite of the great world. It is soon evident to the reader that Chamberlain regarded himself, and wished to be regarded by his friends, as an outsider, a looker-on.[2] He wished no part in the intrigues and manipulations of the pushing men about the Court. He did not laugh at them but he did smile wryly and a little pityingly. His amusement made him the better observer and his disinterestedness was no handicap. That attitude had perhaps been developed when as a sick boy he had watched rather than participated in what was going on, and it had become habitual

[1] To paraphrase Scripture was later regarded at Oxford and Cambridge as the height of the humorous.

[2] Chamberlain prided himself on being a looker-on. Many men of the time regarded themselves as such, seeking the contemplative rather than the active life. Edmund Spenser in a sonnet to his friend, Gabriel Harvey, called him happy above the happiest men:

> that, sitting like a looker-on
> Of this world's stage, doest note with critique pen
> The sharp dislike of each condition.

with the grown man.[1] By the time his record of events began he had worked out a formula satisfactory to himself:

> I am past all ambition and wish nor seek nothing but how to live *suaviter* and in plenty.

In London a looker-on could occupy himself. The metropolis of England was not so large but that one could recognize many of its figures; one could even keep tab on those who came to town to see their lawyers or to pick up talk of the Court and of Parliament. Chamberlain could observe the operations of the great merchants, the schemings of politicians, and the swelling ways of the courtiers. He could watch younger sons getting a start and eldest sons falling in debt; he could mark industrious apprentices becoming city merchants and aldermanic families allying themselves with the county. Were he a philosopher – and Chamberlain was not without philosophy – he could catch the sad rhythm of fortune and the individual. He could gaze on would-be riders to fortune mounting their horses and then perhaps falling from them and being trampled upon,[2] only to be replaced by new men willing to take their chances of being thrown. The game of now up and now down was played at a fast clip. The men who really enjoyed it were the observers and even they must often have shivered at what they saw.

Chamberlain may not have enjoyed it all, but London was in his blood. He came honestly by his attachment to the City. His father, Richard Chamberlain, ironmonger and alderman, was one of those capable tradesmen who shared in the abundance of

[1] Many years before, he had written to Stephen Powle (Tanner MSS., 309, ff.300-1) about one seeking office and honour. 'He must work himself into the world and not tarry till he be called, or modesty is grown out of fashion, and therefore he must become more bold and audacious, yea and somewhat importunate. Perhaps you will say this is against his nature, but this is the way, for so Daniel Rogers crept in, who by report is as fit for that place as I to be Pope . . . A man of worth would disdain to be outshouldered by such companions.'

[2] 'When men are down the very drunkards make rhymes and songs upon them.' II, 40.

Tudor times, becoming Sheriff of London and twice Master of the Worshipful Company of Ironmongers. John's was a double heritage of business people, for his mother was Anne, daughter of Robert Downe, likewise an ironmonger and alderman. Richard and Anne had eleven children, eight of whom survived infancy. The mother died in 1562, when John was eight, and the father, after providing his brood with a stepmother, died four years later. A certain prescience regarding his son John suggests that he was understanding in human as well as in business matters. Because John had been 'tender, sickly and weak', he specified that he was to be brought up to learning, either in the university or in some place beyond the sea, and he commended him to his loving and friendly cousin, Thomas Goore, who was to have the 'bringing him up'.

It is not known whether Chamberlain went to live with Goore, a member of the Grocers' Company and a merchant famous for his hospitality, at his house near St. Mary's, Woolwich, or whether he continued to live at his stepmother's house in the Old Jewry, where his eldest brother, Robert, was master. At sixteen he matriculated at Trinity College, Cambridge, where he stayed long enough to make some life-long friends, and not long enough to take a degree. Probably he went from there direct to Gray's Inn, and tarried there long enough to be reckoned a member of that honourable society, but not long enough to become a barrister.

So far as we know he took up no occupation. Three brothers followed their father's calling, each in turn becoming a Master of the Ironmongers' Company, but John had no inclination that way. He lived a quiet, easy-going, bachelor's life. Towards the end of his life he wrote:

> It hath pleased God still so to deal with me and so to temper my fortune that as I did never abound so I was never in want.

He never married or even set up housekeeping (save once for a few months), preferring to live with relatives or friends, keeping a man to look after his personal needs, and taking his meals with the family or at some tavern with cronies. He lived always within a comfortable walk of St. Paul's. In 1596 he was lodging with Sir William Gilbert, physician and author of the first treatise on magnetism. The pleasant society at that house was broken up in 1604 when Gilbert was appointed physician to the Queen, and Chamberlain moved to the house of another friend, Mark Ridley, likewise a physician. Eventually he settled in the home of his brother, Richard, in Aldermanbury and there, a five minutes' walk from St. Paul's, he lived most of the rest of his life. Richard's death in 1624 left John for a brief period in charge of his own domestic establishment, but finding it too chargeable and troublesome, he asked his nephew and heir, Hugh Windham, to take it over, and continued as before, a lodger.

Chamberlain appears to have been in Paris with his friend, Stephen Powle, in 1579 and was probably again in France in 1581. It was possibly between those dates that he was up and down Italy and gained some knowledge of the people and the language. Later, after Carleton became Ambassador at Venice, he accompanied him there and spent a year with him. On his way back from Venice, he visited German libraries as a respectful pilgrim. In general, however, he was little given to travel and possibly never saw his own England beyond the counties within easy reach of London. Again and again his friend, Carleton, tried to induce him to visit him at The Hague, but Carleton wrote as if he had no real hope that Chamberlain would accept his invitation. A few country visits a year, never further afield than Oxfordshire, interrupted the simple routine of his life. He enjoyed his friends, his leisure, his food, his books, and above all, his news and gossip. To live '*suaviter* and in plenty' became an end in itself, though neither his temperament nor his income encouraged sybaritic indulgence. His independence and his chance to be quiet and methodical were precious to him. A little set in his ways he no doubt became, for he was no lover of 'huddling haste', nor a 'friend to sudden notions'.

Chamberlain had a definite circle of friends which in 1608 he alluded to as 'a whole knot of good fellowship'. Most of the members of that group seem to have been well acquainted with one another, as their letters prove. Just how the fellowship grew up we do not know but it had a nucleus at least as early as 1587. Two of the group, Sir Michael Dormer of Ascott in Oxfordshire, and Samuel Backhouse of Swallowfield, Berkshire, were more or less contemporaries of Chamberlain at Cambridge and may first have known him there. As early as 1587 Chamberlain seems to have been on friendly terms with Thomas Bodley, diplomat and later founder of Bodley's Library, with Peter Evers, a north country gentleman, with Rowland Lytton of Knebworth, Hertfordshire, with William Gent of Oxford, and with Thomas Allen, mathematician and antiquary. It was probably at a later date that Chamberlain came to know Dudley Carleton and Ralph Winwood, who were to prove his two most intimate friends. Carleton was younger than most of the circle but seems to have been on good terms with many of them, whether through Chamberlain or not, I cannot tell. It may very well be that Carleton was introduced to Chamberlain through Rowland Lytton. It is possible that Bodley had been the intermediary between Chamberlain and Winwood. When and how Sir William Borlase of Bockmer, Buckinghamshire, became part of the 'knot', I do not know. The diplomat, Sir Thomas Edmondes, was not, I suspect, quite a member of the circle but was a friend of several of the group and may have come to know Chamberlain through Winwood or Bodley. Among others whom Chamberlain reckoned as friends were Lancelot Andrewes, who had been his contemporary at Cambridge and was eventually to be Bishop of Winchester, William Camden, the historian, and Inigo Jones, the architect and maker of masques.

That circle was not the highest in the country nor in London, but one made up of interesting men and men agreeable to Chamberlain, who did not cultivate the well-known figures of the Court and who would not have felt at home with them. As the years went by, however, when Dudley Carleton, Ralph Winwood and Lancelot Andrewes began to be men of mark, he could not wholly avoid the society of the highly placed. Those men did not forget him. A pleasant gentleman who sought nothing for himself and who was well informed was an asset to an ambassador, a secretary of state, or a bishop.

Chamberlain met his friends at their homes in the country, at their town houses, and at taverns. At the Mermaid in Bread Street, where Ben Jonson and no doubt Shakespeare were seen,[1] Chamberlain once dined with Winwood, Edmondes, Carleton's brother George and William Gent. They drank the health of Carleton and provided better for his than for their own, for Chamberlain wrote that he had been distempered ever since. From such feasts men came away sometimes pretty well whittled, as Chamberlain put it. As the years brought changes Chamberlain dined at Sir Ralph Winwood's, then Secretary of State, along with Lady Arundel, Lady Grey of Ruthven, Lady Wood, Sir Thomas Tracy and Sir Horace Vere. This time Chamberlain felt out of his element, talking with great ladies whom he professed at other times to avoid. Conversation was probably less gay than

[1] If Chamberlain did not know Ben Jonson, he had friends who did. There is no mention of Shakespeare in any letter of Chamberlain's. Chamberlain was ten years older than Shakespeare. When Shakespeare came to London at about twenty-three, Chamberlain would have been thirty-three. The actor-playwright lived, of course, even after he attained some position in his world, in a milieu very different from that of Chamberlain, though they may easily have met at taverns. Chamberlain would hardly have been interested in an actor, or even in a rising young dramatist who was well liked in his circle. What is more important is that they lived in the same centre and heard much the same news, although Chamberlain no doubt had better access to news.

at the Mermaid,[1] but the dinner seems to have agreed better with Chamberlain. Never had he seen so good a feast for so small a company. Much as he liked good talk he was not averse to good food.

He had other diversions. Masques and plays he was usually content to hear about from friends. Once indeed to please Lady Cope he acted as chaperon to her daughter, Isobel, and Sir Rowland Lytton's 'huswives' at a play and found himself as weary as they were wanton. Perhaps the young women were a shade too lively for the sedate bachelor:

> All the comfort I had was that my Lady Cope said she would not commit her daughter to any man's care but mine.

He was the serviceable old bachelor, a dependable escort. With Lady Fanshawe, Lady Cope, Isobel Cope and the daughter of Lord Norris he made an expedition to the Copes' new house in Kensington, later to be Holland House, where early-nineteenth-century political society gathered and listened to Macaulay holding forth. The place, Chamberlain reported, was in readiness for inspection by the Queen and while the guests could look their fill they could not touch so much as a cherry. Or perhaps he went to Fulham a-shroving and came home laden with sweetmeats.

[1] No doubt at such dinners Chamberlain picked up some of his information about affairs. Massinger in *The City Madam* (Act II, Scene 1) makes Luke describe the glories of dinners of the great:

> Then sitting at the table with
> The braveries of the kingdom, you shall hear
> Occurrents from all corners of the world,
> The plots, the counsels, the designs of princes,
> And freely censure them.

Massinger was probably thinking of men's dinners. I suspect that at the dinners of men and women the conversation was rather formal.

II

Chamberlain was in his forties when he began news-gathering for Dudley Carleton. An old acquaintance of the Carleton family, he was interested in the promising young man twenty years his junior, and had fallen in the way of writing to him even before Carleton went abroad. When Carleton crossed the Channel nothing was more natural than that Chamberlain should let him know what was happening. Often he wrote literally post-haste when the wind on the Channel was favourable, and a messenger waited at the door for the letter to be finished. During the long vacation the correspondence was likely to lag, but even then Chamberlain might have gossip to report about members of his and Carleton's own circle.

He wrote with freedom and enjoined upon Carleton the necessity of keeping his communications to himself, explaining that he was so used to liberty and freedom of speech in conversation that he could not give it up in writing.

We may imagine that both Chamberlain and Carleton in their rather closed group of intimates had been accustomed to talking with a certain freedom. Writing was another matter. 'Many things are spoken', wrote Chamberlain, 'that are not to be written.' Even spoken words might land one in the Tower or involve one in a duel. But letters that went through several hands on their way and might be tampered with could easily cause their writers trouble. Moreover letters were in that day passed around to kin and friends. Chamberlain and Carleton seem to have developed, however, a technique of making innocuous statements that nevertheless carried overtones. One could phrase a matter so that it seemed harmless enough to anyone but those who understood the background. Moreover both men must have been scrupulous in what they showed to others, for neither ever complained of any violation of confidence.

Chamberlain had a sense of responsibility for what he wrote. He picked up information from many types of people and he had to use judgment in sifting what he heard, in discriminating between fact and fancy. His friend, Ned Wymark, was always telling him stories, but Chamberlain and the recipient of his letters understood that Ned's gossip was to be taken with reserve.

So was much other gossip. Chamberlain would put in his letters warnings that such and such a report might not be true. Typical of the rumours was the report received in late 1602 that the French king had been slain by a friar. It was 'very current and took fire like a train or squib'. Chamberlain's calm incredulity and his scrupulousness in correcting gossip that turned out to be ill founded were excellent attributes for a purveyor of news.[1]

The historian must be grateful not only for Chamberlain's pains to be accurate, but also for his subtle expression of the various moods of the time. Himself given to ups and downs of spirit, he was sensitive to the waves of feeling of his time. When his letters began in 1597 the English were still recalling the glories of the victory over Spain in 1588 and were confident that the Queen and her ministers could pilot them through whatever dangers might be ahead. The sovereign that succeeded Elizabeth did not inspire the same confidence. Yet as long as Robert Cecil, 'the great little lord', carried on with his cautious control, Chamberlain and his countrymen were not too dissatisfied. When Cecil died and the Elizabethan age became a memory the public mood changed. Men lost what had meant much to them, the expectancy of great events. 'The calmness of this age breeds little alteration', complained the Paul's-walker when Cecil's term

[1] In 1619 Chamberlain was a witness in a suit brought by Lady Winwood against John More, who had been a steward for Sir Ralph Winwood. Chamberlain was anxious to support Lady Winwood as far as he could but he was stating matters with great care, testifying only what he was certain he could remember. He was indeed an impressive witness. See P.R.O., c. 24/461/143.

was nearly run, and the calmness was not welcome, nor the peace with Spain, nor the kingcraft of the royal bungler.

In the years following Cecil's death Chamberlain's disillusionment with the world he watched must have been increasingly apparent to Carleton. The satirists of the time were fond of speaking of manors thrown away upon clothes. It was a money-minded and pretentious generation. The worth of a woman's ring, or of her headgear, or of her coronet, was stated in flat terms. The Lady Wotton had a gown that cost her £50 a yard for the embroidery. 'This extreme cost and riches makes us all poor', commented Chamberlain.

He became more depressed as he watched little men and grasping families directing affairs. Nobility of character and weighty and worthy purposes seemed out of fashion. Gradually his uneasiness betrayed itself in quiet complaint or in nostalgia for the old days. In 1620 he marked a fatal *fainéantise* and barrenness of the time and was obviously fearful of what might follow. He could not foresee the shouting apprentices outside the House of Lords in 1641 nor the crowd that dark January day in 1649, silent before Whitehall. But he did realize that the merry and mighty England of his earlier manhood was no more. Little there was to quicken his step or foster his pride of Englishry.

Fortunately he had much to do for Carleton besides writing letters and expressing moods. Carleton gave him errands to do and those errands brought him many connections but entailed waiting in the ante-rooms of the great.

There had been a time immediately after the Gunpowder Plot (November 1605) when waiting was not pleasant, when the cautious Cecil kept Carleton in suspense. An untoward circumstance, the fact that Carleton had been secretary to Henry Percy, ninth Earl of Northumberland, who was unjustly suspected of having had a hand in the conspiracy, made Carleton temporarily unsuitable for employment in His Majesty's service. He was called back from Paris and was for a short time under confinement. He was discouraged about the outlook for his future and went so far as to write to the Earl asking that he might be a farmer on one of the Earl's farms. A friend advised him to pick contentment from books,[1] and he seriously also considered returning to Oxford as a scholar. His letters betrayed a quiet desperation which worried his associates. Chamberlain was more philosophical and wrote to him:

> I see you must bear of this storm as well as you may, and ride it out at anchor, till the weather grow more calm.

Carleton was a bit unreasonable in his answer:

> If you think best that ... I should ride it out, you must provide me some such good anchor hold, or else you may consider my peril.[2]

The weather did grow more calm. Carleton was presently released from custody and restored to some slight degree of favour. It was still necessary to keep his name before Cecil. It was believed that one way of getting at that powerful figure was through Sir Walter Cope, a belief that Cope did not discourage. In his letters Chamberlain dubbed Cope 'the idle oracle of the Strand',[3] but went out of his way nevertheless to call upon him and to keep Carleton's interests before him. Cope was worth propitiating even at the expense of those presents and services which such intermediaries expected. It was best, Chamberlain believed, to hold a candle before a devil, not for his help but lest he do harm.

Chamberlain carried out other commissions for Carleton, who at length had been given a post abroad. Carleton would send him a gift for such and such a lady and ask him to pay a bill for him, or to inform someone that Carleton was not neglecting his interests.

[1] Carleton to Chamberlain, July 4th, 1606. S.P. 14/22, No. 29.
[2] Carleton to Chamberlain, November 23rd, 1606. S.P. 78/47, f. 204.
[3] Cope was a talented and a not unimaginative man; he had influence with Cecil.

Once indeed Carleton offered to put Chamberlain in the way of a little windfall. Carleton hoped to secure for a friend a small secretaryship in Ireland once promised to him, and he had agreed to accept £400 available for use in gaining the post. If Chamberlain through his influence with Winwood (by that time Secretary of State) could secure the secretaryship for Carleton's friend, he might pocket £300. 'It is *honestum lucrum*,' wrote Carleton, 'and will never lie heavy upon your conscience, for bribery, I know you are very scrupulous.'

III

Chamberlain's life was so involved with that of Carleton that something must be said about the latter. Carleton was a younger son of an Oxfordshire family and had done well at Christ Church. He is of course much better known to history than Chamberlain; his ambassadorships are part of the record of English foreign affairs in his time; he became during the early years of Charles I an important member of the Government and was created Lord Dorchester. With such matters we are not concerned here; we would know what kind of a man it was to whom Chamberlain wrote and to whom he was so closely attached.

In his earlier years Carleton sent a letter to Chamberlain about once a fortnight, except when they both happened to be in London or staying at the same house in the country. Later, as his diplomatic duties became onerous, he wrote about once a month. He recognized what he owed to Chamberlain, who through the influence of Winwood had helped him get his first small job in the English embassy at Paris:[1]

[1] Yet he recognized that others had a part in giving him his start, as Sir Edward Phelips (Phelips MSS., H.M.C., III, 281). It would appear that Edmondes also had some part in gaining Carleton his first appointment in Paris. See Birch, *An Historical View o the Negotiations* (London, 1749), p. 203.

> I must [page torn] you to be the first which set me going in this course and have seen, guided, and upheld me by your good counsels and encouragements, when I have been often sinking for want of breath and giving over in plain field.

He put it more subtly by referring to leaf 551 of Michel de Montaigne, in his chapter *De l'affection des pères aux enfants*, 'where', he wrote, 'we are painted to the life'.[1] In many letters he asked advice of his mentor as to his next move. Should he leave Paris at once where he felt that the English ambassador was treating him badly, or should he go on blindly and try the worst that could happen?

Chamberlain's reply was indecisive. He was sparing of advice but, when pressed, was given to the counsel of patience. In this instance, however, he went to the trouble of consulting Carleton's brother, his cousin, Sir Rowland Lytton, and Sir Thomas Edmondes, putting before them the situation as Carleton presented it.

> To tell you truly, methinks we are like physicians that consult of a patient without feeling any part of his pain, and finding the disease somewhat difficult, apply no other remedy but good words and good wishes, and make him believe that time and good diet will cure it alone.

The two men wrote letters that were not unlike in the topics treated, and even in the handwriting. Carleton once complained to Chamberlain that much of what he heard was not worth imparting, 'the humour of the time being spent in discourse of quarrels and marriages',[2] but he himself could deal out gossip with the best of them and serve it indeed with a flourish. Like Chamberlain he viewed the foibles of his friends charitably but was less lenient about those of others. He was less of a news-

[1] Carleton to Chamberlain, June 8th, 1602. S.P. 78/16, f. 100.
[2] Carleton to Chamberlain, December 25th, 1606. S.P. 14/24, No. 29.

gatherer than Chamberlain but he was glad of every item Chamberlain sent him.[1] In one instance writing from London to Edmondes in Paris he lifted several sentences and a whole paragraph from a spicy letter he had just received from Chamberlain. The two men had the same nickname for those about the Court. Signor Fabritio, for example, was Sir Henry Wotton.

Of course Carleton's letters, after he became a proper diplomat, were more devoted to what was going on in Europe, in Paris, in Venice, or at The Hague, wherever he happened to be stationed, than those of Chamberlain, who was writing usually from London. Towards the end of a letter, however, Carleton would mention the various Englishmen who were in the vicinity, in town, or staying with him, or were on their way to visit him, or had just left him for some other court, or for England. The Countess of Pembroke, the Earl of Arundel and his wife, who were going round Europe collecting pictures and statuary with the help of Inigo Jones; this and that ambassador or former ambassador, Sir Dudley Digges, Sir Isaac Wake or Sir Horace Vere; business men over from London looking after the interests of London companies and looking over the accounts of their factors; Sir Arthur Ingram, the John D. Rockefeller of his time; all of them Carleton mentioned. If he were in Venice when they passed through, he saw to it that they were introduced to the people they wished to meet. At The Hague he performed the same functions for English visitors. For the merchants who had complaints to make about injustices done them in trading he did what he could, and reported his efforts to London.

About continental affairs Carleton told Chamberlain largely what he could presently learn from other sources. Occasionally he warned Chamberlain not to know what he had told him until he heard it from others. Carleton was discretion itself and seldom

[1] He once wrote to Chamberlain: 'Your plenty is so well sauced with judicious choice and variety that fasting or full stomach your letters are ever most welcome.' October 19th, 1600. S.P. 12/275, f. 189.

discussed diplomatic moves and knew that he could trust Chamberlain.

Chamberlain must have found Carleton an uneasy correspondent. Sir Dudley worried too much. Chamberlain wrote to him:

> You need not take things so to heart, for such matters are no longer thought on than they are in speech, and therefore to mention them is to revive them, and the best means to have them forgotten is to forget first and bury all in silence, for good words and bad words pass away like water that runs apace.

Carleton was not only a worrier but exceedingly temperamental. He wrote to Chamberlain:

> I trouble all my friends with my private [affairs] as if I were of that moment that all the world were interested and did labour in my behalf.[1]

He realized his own self-absorption and yet had criticized others for that fault. He was always restless, looking ahead to the next post, and unable to live happily in the present. As an attaché in Paris in 1602 he had disliked his work, which was probably little more than the transcription of letters. Even when, much later, he had become an ambassador at Venice, and later still at The Hague, he regarded his office, which he never neglected, as a stepping stone to a secretaryship to the King or to some equivalent job in London. He expected Chamberlain and his other friends to be on the look-out for all vacancies and to use what influence on his behalf they could. At the same time he did not wish the notion to get abroad that he was unhappy in his present position lest someone step into his shoes and he go barefoot. In his discouragement at the outlook ahead he would pretend that he did not care what happened, 'for fall back or fall edge, it maketh no great matter'.

[1] Carleton to Chamberlain, November 23rd, 1602. S.P. 78/47, f. 204.

No easy task was that of Chamberlain to watch out for possible openings for his friend and protégé and yet betray no impression of dissatisfaction on Carleton's part. In writing to Carleton he was never enthusiastic about Carleton's chances; indeed he was likely to indicate that for the moment his chances were not good. He was a frank rather than an optimistic friend.

In 1623, when Carleton was coming close to his long-hoped-for appointment in London but did not realize it, he wrote rather pathetically to Chamberlain:

> It is no small pleasure to find friends at a time of need but that hath been my fate of late years only to have use of friends to keep me from heart. I hope God will one day send me some to do me good.

In those sentences he was less than fair to his friends.

In his discontent with his exile on the Continent Carleton was not alone among ambassadors. His Majesty's servants abroad were nearly always homesick. Carleton wrote to Trumbull about a friend:

> I shall envy him that shall be nearer the air of England and that he shall have God's dear earth under his feet.[1]

The diplomatic agents of England regarded their assignments as away from the main line of promotion. When the plums were dropping the men under the tree were likely to pick them up. Faithful service abroad was sometimes praised but usually forgotten when the favours were being distributed.

Carleton missed the good talk of London. Once when Chamberlain wrote that he had not availed himself recently of his acquaintance with Lancelot Andrewes, then Bishop of Ely and one of the best minds in England, Carleton answered him wistfully:

[1] In the same tone Stephen Powle wrote to Edward Egerton in 1588: 'And the shadow of an English oak would give me a more perfect refreshing to my whole body than the stately pines of Ravenna.' Tanner MSS., 309, f. 57v.

SIR DUDLEY CARLETON, 1ST VISCOUNT DORCHESTER

> If you had been penned up for so many years together as now I have been, from changing almost a word with any man of merit, unless it be with a public minister (whose conversation consists only of compliment), or a straggling traveller (who hath no more for you than he gathers from the highway), you would know what it is to lose so good an opportunity.

The travellers who dropped in at the Embassy, diplomats going their appointed ways, young men of family doing the grand tour, and elderly gentlemen of gravity and of formal language, did not always afford intellectual refreshment.

Carleton was not wholly given over to moodiness. He relished gaiety of spirits in his friends and sometimes exhibited it himself.[1] He liked to recall merry occasions with his friends and the old days in the House of Commons when he and his circle there had been conspirators together. He was vastly entertained when he ran into a group of gentlewomen, 'mad wenches', proceeding from one house to another with a concert of musicians. He was amused when he saw Sir Sprintado (a nickname for some pompous man) with a handbow in his hand hunting in little Lister's park. At Knebworth on a vist to his kinsman, Lytton, one of his liveliest companions, he wrote to Chamberlain:

> Here lacks nothing but your good company to make up a merry Christmas, for though there be no great solemnity, nor piping, nor dancing, yet the cards talk at all hours, and we lack not tales by the fireside. Besides we make war upon the blackbirds with birding pieces and even now I came from overthrowing of a doe with the same weapon. You will be remembered tomorrow at the eating of it, as you are not long forgotten at anything where a friend were to be wished. Let

[1] He had a feeling for nature. He loved the country, the 'apricocks' growing, and the changes of seasons.

us hear at least how the world goes in London and if it be true, as was told us this day, that the Thames is frozen over, to make up the miracles of our King's reign, then let the world slide, for so it may with conveniency.

Gay, moody, self-absorbed and self-seeking, Carleton treated Chamberlain almost as a spoiled son might treat an indulgent father. In his quotation from Montaigne he had suggested that the relationship was somewhat like that of father and son. Carleton expected much as his due, and gave little. As for Chamberlain he was satisfied to take the younger friend on his own terms. He asked no *quid pro quo*.

IV

Politics, Carleton's ambitions, and the gossip of a close-knit circle were only part of what the two men had in common. They were linked by Chamberlain's interest in Carleton's relatives. Carleton's sisters furnished Chamberlain with continuous matter for discussion. Long hours and patience he devoted to dissuading them from succumbing to the blandishments of the Catholics. In his efforts he was supported by their brother who had less patience with them.[1] One of them, Bridget, who was later to marry Sir Hercules Underhill (then pronounced Undrill), became infatuated with a Catholic who had won her affections by his fiddling. 'A fiddlesticks for him', Carleton wrote. Chamberlain thought of her as a peevish and wilful creature. Carleton found the sisters fantastical, and was inclined to talk of the inconstancy of women, until he bethought himself of his saintly mother who had brought up the daughters in a religious course and had been ill rewarded. He wished his Catholic, apostolical sister would

[1] All the sisters seem to have been given to moodiness and quarrelsomeness. Carleton himself we would today call an 'edgy' person.

take less care for a ghostly father and betake herself to a bodily husband.[1] Elizabeth Carleton, who had married Alexander Williams, met with more approval.

But there was Alice, whom Chamberlain in a letter to Carleton called 'your wisest and best esteemed sister', the favourite of both Chamberlain and of Carleton. To her Chamberlain sent occasional chatty epistles somewhat the same as those to her brother, but perhaps more given up to marriages, births, expected events, and the gowns worn at the last masque than to the weighty problems as to who was and who was not slated for office. It has been suggested by Norman McClure, whose scholarship is characterized by much common sense, that an allusion by Chamberlain in his will to Alice may mean that he and Alice had planned marriage. In that document Chamberlain wrote:

> This I do, in regard of the sincere goodwill and honest affection I bear her, and of the true and long-continued friendship between us, and for a testimony of that further good I had intended to her, if God had given me means.

Moreover there is a letter of Carleton's, which I shall quote later, about an unhappy woman who had been confiding to him about her affair with Chamberlain. McClure suggests that the woman was Alice. The possible romance between Chamberlain and Alice Carleton may seem to the reader hardly worth pursuing, but it does afford us a few clues as to Chamberlain.

I am inclined to guess that Chamberlain had once thought of marriage with Alice and had long since given it up. In 1594 his friend, Stephen Powle, had composed a letter to him, a letter he seems never to have sent off, in which he recalled their walks and talks in France together and Chamberlain's many asseverations at that time (1579) that he was never going to marry, asseverations often made. Now in 1594 Powle had learned that his friend was

[1] Carleton to . . . S.P. 78/46, f. 71.

about to marry and was full of felicitations. It is the merest conjecture that at that time Chamberlain had been interested in Alice. If he had been, he may have thought better of it. She was poor, and seventeenth-century gentlemen liked to have their brides bring something in their stockings. Chamberlain had enough to live on comfortably, as a single man, but not enough perhaps in his judgment to set up a household. In 1598, four years later, Chamberlain had written to Carleton that Alice was in the country, and 'belike there is somewhat brewing', and Carleton had answered him that he hoped the matter would 'come to a tapping'.[1] Chamberlain did not write as one deeply concerned but as a well-wishing friend. Somewhat later he became worried about her Catholic tendencies. In 1603 he wrote to Carleton that Alice was taken in the same trap as Bridget (her sister), that is, in the Catholic trap,

> so that I see if wenches have not their will and that husbands come not at call we shall have them all discontented and turn Turk.

If he had earlier considered marriage with Alice he had long since given up such an idea.

At the time of which I have been writing Chamberlain was in his late forties, a bachelor rather set in his ways, probably still playing with the idea of marriage but shying away when his friends tried to interest him. There is an episode in his life at this time that has the authentic marks of an old bachelor of his time of life. We learn about it from a letter that his intimate friend, Sir Rowland Lytton, wrote to him from Knebworth in 1605:

> I am not satisfied with your answer concerning the widow. I will not give over replying till you rejoin. It was told me that her estate was 4000*li*, if it be but 3000*li* take out the writ of *habeas corpus cum causa* and join in issue without any more

[1] May 28th-June 6th, 1598. S.P. 12/267, f. 90.

ado. You have already gone through the whole course of the bachelor's boat, and are at the pergola [i.e. high stand] of all the pleasures of a single life. You say you grow melancholy, neither do you often meet with company to your mind. You love not to go abroad, and you find not home to your liking. When therefore so cheerful a change of life presents a new recreation, so good encouragement of party and portion offers itself, and the certainty of former liking gives assurance of a constant happiness, what skuse [excuse] can you make to withstand so good a fortune. Remember how you are left alone and we have all forsaken you, Sir Walter Cope, Sir Hugh Beeston, Sir Peter Eure [Evers], Sir William Borlase, S. Backhouse. Will you be an heretic or do you think all these honest men are gone to hell? No, no. Purgatory is the worst and that you may endure with patience a little in respect of former venial sins, but if they be in heaven, as charity bindeth you to think, what case stand you in then? Repent in time and forsake the solitary eagle's life, go pair with the dove, and send me a new pair of gloves, and if, upon a twelve month's trial you disallow my counsel I will fetch for you ten flitches of bacon from Dunmow.[1]

When I first lit upon this letter I was surprised to find a widow in Chamberlain's life. I might have guessed as much. The old bachelor, now turned fifty, was still playing with the thought of marriage and his friends understood him well enough to fear that he would not follow through.

Less than a year later Carleton wrote a letter to Chamberlain which may bear on the same matter:

[1] I suspect Sir Rowland submitted a copy of this letter to Carleton after sending it to Chamberlain. On the margin it is marked *Stet* in a hand that looks like that of Carleton. In an undated letter of Carleton to Chamberlain (S.P. 14/24, No. 36) he says: 'I have sent you your paper which I may even now say I have overread, and taken no small pleasure in a review of the old world, amongst others this one here inclosed I took particular note of, which I send you by itself that you may, if you please, read it again and consider how well you are therein counselled.'

I was yesterday sent unto by a good friend of yours (who was left at home *in solitudine*) to come and see her, and she well cummered [cumbered] me with so many tears that I wished I had saved my journey. I am so tender-hearted that I cannot but suffer with so good a friend; and I did likewise bear a part in that unusual sadness I observed in you at our two last meetings. I might ask why should affection produce this effect? Why should you discontent yourselves the nearer you come to that issue, which I have ever thought you intended for both your contentments, but I may answer myself by the common custom, *bellum pax rursum*, and I hope these wars will soon be at an end. I have somewhat to say to you from the melancholy party. . . .

Now Carleton can hardly have been talking about his sister, Alice, as Norman McClure suspects. He would not have referred to her as 'so good a friend', or at least he would have intimated that the relationship was not only one of friendship. Furthermore, he and Chamberlain both knew Alice's temper and her leaning towards Rome, and had taken those weaknesses very seriously. If Carleton had been really trying to persuade his friend to marry his sister, he would surely have said something to indicate that those facts were really insignificant and that Chamberlain might well overlook them.[1] Moreover it is hard to believe that the lady who was so full of tears was that Alice whose romance with Chamberlain, if there had been one, was old stuff.[2] Is it not much more probable that Carleton was discussing the widow whom Lytton had implored him to marry?

About three years later, Carleton in a letter to Chamberlain implies that Chamberlain is about to undertake a 'change of place

[1] It is to be said that the phrase 'those wars', used by Carleton in his letter about the unhappy woman, could refer to the old troubles between Chamberlain and Alice.

[2] See Chamberlain to Carleton (February 17th, 1614) about Alice then in Venice with her brother, and her unhappiness and possible decision.

and course of life'. Was Carleton alluding to a proposed marriage? Was Chamberlain still involved with the widow? Or was he now interested in someone else? I have examined the letters to make a guess as to who the widow might have been, or who the someone else might be. I can find no satisfactory clue. The widow may well have been someone Chamberlain never talked about. We shall hardly find out who she was.[1] We may be allowed to guess that Chamberlain lost his nerve at the end.

Did he ever regret his unmarried state? In 1615 he wrote of his discontent with travel, 'being grown so in love with home (or that which I make account of as home)'.

Once in speaking of financial transactions and possible investments Chamberlain called himself 'withal so timorous'. Timorous he was, as his letters abundantly indicate. He was more than that. He was wanting in initiative. He did not plan his own life. He accepted invitations to the country because he was asked. In general he was likely to do what his friends suggested to him. Marriage was a great step, even when his friends urged it upon him, and he always drew back.

Late in 1605 there seems to have been another quarrel between him and Alice. She became very angry at something he had said, words which he readily admitted were unadvised and idle on his part. But he felt and told her that she had made too great a fuss about them. He believed that, considering his long endeavours on her part (of twice seven years)[2] he had been badly treated. He wrote to her:

[1] Twice in his last years Chamberlain referred to the Lady Wake as his ancient valentine (II, 495, 603). She had not been a widow when she married Wake. In his later years Chamberlain saw her often and was on good terms with her.

[2] An obvious allusion to Jacob's fourteen years' service for Rachel. The words would seem to imply that Chamberlain had long sought her hand. Yet I suspect the quarrel was about her leanings towards Catholicism. Moreover seven years earlier he had written of what seems to have been a marriage possibility for Alice (if we may judge from his guarded words). The more I read the letter the more I believe his twice seven years meant nothing more than his devotion to her interests. None of his letters to her or those in which he mentions her are those of one in love with her. They seem the letters of an elderly friend who wishes her well.

> Patience is the poor man's virtue (though no poor virtue), wherewith I will arm myself to bear out this banishment, which I hope I shall do the better, for that I grow weary of these domestical wars and factious wranglings there among you.

The other side of the story we do not know, but it is clear that Chamberlain regarded her as excitable, like her sister. In the same year there is a letter in which her brother wrote earnestly, if affectionately, begging her to give up her passionate temper. That she did not give it up and was later angry at her brother is evident from one of Chamberlain's letters to Carleton.

Alice Carleton became in due course that rather unusual specimen in her time, a middle-aged spinster. 'Your nun sister', Chamberlain calls her in one of his letters to her brother. Whatever Chamberlain had against her he continued to write letters to her and left her at his death an annuity of £80 and £600 in money, his carved chest with its contents, and anything of his then in her possession. His bequest was no doubt welcome; Carleton's wife had spoken of her as 'very poor and very proud'.

V

When the term was over most of Chamberlain's friends rode to the country. Chamberlain betook himself to one of the several country houses where he and Carleton had friends in common, some of them Carleton's kin. To no seat was he more likely to go than to Knebworth, where Lyttons lived (and still lived until a few years ago), a house with much good company of pictures and discourses. Sir Rowland Lytton was a member of the House of Commons and had friends in high places, but seems to have exerted himself little to get on. Of him Carleton declared that he knew not a better mind in a weaker body. At his best he was a merry old soul who deserved his circle of friends. Chamberlain spoke of his letters as 'merry and gamesome', and may have been thinking of the letter in which Lytton urged him to marry. Other letters were just as spirited. When Carleton married the young widow of Sir Walter Treadway and was expecting an heir, Sir Rowland wrote him gleefully:

> I joy to see, though dim of sight, that you have done your lady right, above the valour of her former knight, in the adventures of the night.

When he was urging Chamberlain to visit him he wrote:

> Come you and Dudley over . . . fear not lodging; he shall have the new chamber and you and I will ligg [lie] in bed together. Say the word when the horse shall come.

Chamberlain did often say the word. There was little resisting Sir Rowland. Every summer Chamberlain would be off to Knebworth, and, much as he disliked winter visiting, would share the Lytton Christmas-New Year's festivities. Lady Lytton was one of the women whom both he and Carleton admired. At Knebworth there was not a great deal of regular entertainment save bowling, hunting and hawking.

At times Chamberlain rode from Knebworth into Hampshire to stay with the Wallops at Farleigh (where Wallops still live) where Lytton's daughter was mistress. If such tours furnished him little news they supplied him with homely gossip which was almost equally welcome to Carleton. Thus in October of 1601 he found his Hampshire circle astir with domestic events. He arrived at Farleigh for the churching of Lady Wallop, who had a new son, and then visited her daughter, Winifred, the wife of Sir Richard Gifford of Somborne. Some old joke, too familiar to Carleton to need explanation, led Chamberlain to refer to the young bride as 'my wife'. He was pleased to see how well she was accommodated with all manner of household implements, and he found her playing the housewife 'out of cry' [beyond measure], but feared she would have much ado to bring that riotous and disordered household into any order. Of her success, however, he was the more hopeful because she had so kind and tractable a husband, who made much of her,

> whereof, I take no small comfort and the more for that it is thought she is prettily forward with child, though I need not brag nor boast of it.

A niece and a nephew's wife he found in the same condition, and concluded that it had been 'a gossipping journey and full of increase'.

He was a guest in demand. One cannot read Carleton's letters without discovering Chamberlain's popularity. It is evident that hostesses did what they could to secure him for visits as long as possible. They used Carleton's influence over him; they availed themselves of old promises Chamberlain had made when in an expansive mood. It must not be supposed that he did not enjoy country-house visiting. For all his devotion to London he would have found it hard to forgo his round of visits.

His letters prove how readily he fell into country life. He was going next week into Hertfordshire to take part of the spring. He reported the welcome but ordinary entertainment offered by Sir Edward Norris at Beckley Park, where they coursed and killed but took nothing away, and the plums and melons, and the good fishing of bream and carp to be had at Ascott with the Sir Michael Dormers. True the Dormers had disappointed him by their passion for modernization. They had cut down the trees and defaced the hedges in order to gain better air and wider prospects. He liked the country as it was and had no zest for wider views.

In his later years he spent much time at Ware Park in Hertfordshire with the Fanshawes. 'Mr. Chamberlain is where he would be,' wrote Carleton to a mutual friend, 'at Ware Park.' He entered as fully into the life of the family there as into that of any he visited. Whatever the Fanshawes had in hand, gardening, hunting, or awaiting a family event, he enjoyed with them. In 1606 he had found them in a coil of gardening and he watched things go forward. About forty men were levelling and resetting trees. In the midst of it all Sir Henry was making a fort in perfect proportion with ramparts, bulwarks, counterscarps and all other appurtenances.[1] Chamberlain enjoyed the sweet airs, he listened to the cuckoos, but failed even after a week's effort to hear the nightingales. Sir Henry, who was Remembrancer of the Exchequer, would be off to town; his brother-in-law, Sir Christopher Hatton, and his wife, were leaving too, and Lady Fanshawe was ready to lie down, being so big that she could scarce go up and downstairs.

Seven years later the fort at Ware Park had given way to a fountain, a trout stream was being introduced into the upper garden, and Chamberlain thought it time to call a halt on inventions and changes in a place already pleasant enough. The gardens became so famous for their fruit that the Earl of Arundel and Inigo Jones visited them in 1618 to see the grapes and peaches, and the King asked to be supplied twice a week with that kind of provision.[2]

These people whom Chamberlain visited formed a good cross-section of the better type of gentle families, moderately well-to-do, public-spirited and kindly. Between the lines we can read that they valued Chamberlain's qualities, his common sense, his readiness to appreciate a joke, and, when more brilliant company was present, to efface himself. Who would have known better how

[1] Two months later, just before Christmas, there was still paling, ditching, plashing of hedges, stocking of trees, catching of moles.

[2] Sir John Oglander wrote (*A Royalist Notebook*, p. 196) that James was an infinite lover of fruit, as grapes, melons and the like.

to enliven a wet week-end with his gossip or with episodes drawn out of his experience, who a fitter chaperon for the young people on a visit to neighbours? He had no need or wish to be made a fuss over, content with the affection of his friends.

He was always losing his feminine friends. His niece, Elizabeth Stukely, died in childbed. Mistress Dormer fell sick and Chamberlain wrote sadly: 'if God do call her I shall think this a dismal unlucky year to lose my women friends so fast'. She lived, but Lady Lytton died within a few months after a confinement and her husband Sir Rowland took his loss to heart. Chamberlain could only hope that the approved medicine of time would work as well with him as with others. Chamberlain himself found it hard to digest the solitariness of Knebworth, which was wont to be stirring and cheerful, but believed it would be no good manner to forsake the Lytton family in their solitariness, having always had a part in their pleasures. For three or four years he continued to be an implement of household for Christmas.

When his friends lingered in the country during fine Octobers he missed them. London could be desolate. He would find himself melancholic were it not for the merry progresses he had enjoyed in the country, the memory of which continued to run up and down in his head.

Yet sometimes his mood called for nothing else than solitude. He would refuse to leave London for the pleasure of a winter journey, which was likely to net him little but rheum and the toothache. Or, if he yielded to importunity and went to the country, he would find himself restless. Even at Knebworth, where he had been much at home, particularly as long as Lady Lytton had been alive, he would feel himself tied by the leg. Were it not for an old homage he owed to the house, he confessed to Carleton, he would think every day spent there to be twice lost in his life. His craving for his own company would overcome him. 'Upon some occasions I am grown so private that I stir not abroad, nor mean to do, but to live at home like a snail in the shell.' He had no occupation and no family to take his mind off himself.

He limited himself rather closely to his own narrow circle of families, whom he had long known and whose lives and ways suited his quiet disposition. He was well aware of the wider group whom he called 'the better sort of people', who had a natural right to wealth and power and who bore the responsibility for the orderly conduct of society. They made news and he watched their doings. For the great of the Court and their wives he had little liking. From a covey of such gay company expected at Ware Park he fled as from the plague. City merchants and heads of companies and their wives he seldom mentioned and when he did, it was with just a hint of superiority. He himself had been born into the well-to-do bourgeoisie, but had grown away from them. I am not sure that he recognized their increasing importance in the world in which he lived.

I have devoted some paragraphs to sketching in Chamberlain's circle. It is impossible of course to say precisely what a man owes to his associates but we can understand and appraise him the better if we are familiar with them. It would help us a great deal in appraising him if we could learn what those associates thought of him. We know that Carleton and Lytton were devoted to him Bishop Lancelot Andrewes, who saw the best company in the realm, wrote to Carleton of Chamberlain that he saw him nothing so often as his desire was.[1] Chamberlain's friends liked him well enough to conspire together about him. In 1604 Sir Thomas Edmondes was scheming to turn over his place as a burgess in the House of Commons to Chamberlain, and Carleton wrote Cham-

[1] Andrewes to Carleton, February 24th, 1613. S.P. 14/72, No. 42. Toby Matthews when he returned to London in 1617 asked Carleton to entreat his 'good wise friend, Mr. Chamberlain, to let me clearly and infinitely know from time to time what errors I shall be thought to commit in my behaviour, that I may mend them ere it be too late'. *Court and Times of James I*, II, 22.

berlain that many of his friends would fall out with him if he refused. 'I leave it to Sir Rowland Lytton to tell you there is no denial.'[1] In 1610 Carleton had asked his friend to accompany him to Venice and Sir Thomas Bodley, Sir Rowland Lytton and William Gent had laid their heads together to 'put new life into him', and 'were all persuaders to this journey'.[2] His friends were so fond of him that they went to trouble about him.[3]

What did they say about him when they compared notes? No doubt they had arrived, as groups will do, at a kind of common judgment about their friend, a judgment formulated out of their accumulated observation and refined by the most penetrating of them. The combined verdict thus arrived at may have been generally accepted at the time, but was seldom set down on paper.[4] In that time letters were rather formal and men were likely to be guarded even in their talk. They would not have put into their slowly wrought epistles their comments upon a man's idiosyncrasies.

If one could inquire of Dudley Carleton, of Rowland Lytton, or of Ralph Winwood, about the individual traits of their Paul's-walker friend their reports might take one aback. Perhaps Sir Rowland, if he could revisit this world, as the classical heroes in the books he read sometimes did, and run over this account of his friend, would smile knowingly. He might say (if I may modernize his language): You have been too kind to him. An agreeable

[1] Carleton to Chamberlain, January 15th, 1604. S.P. 14/12, No. 19.

[2] Carleton to Winwood, August 28th, 1610. Winwood, *Memorials*, III, 213.

[3] In 1611 Lytton wrote to Carleton that he had seen Borlase and Backhouse, 'who both have now upon my deliverance of your commendation kindly suspended the expostulatory epistles that were running upon Mr. Chamberlain' (S.P. 14/61, No. 80, February 12th, 1611). That their expostulations were friendly and aimed at Chamberlain's interest we may be reasonably certain.

[4] Occasionally indeed the verdict was set down. It might happen that one of a man's circle was interested in writing character-studies — an interest that developed late in English history — and his study of his friend might be the embodiment of the general opinion of his contemporaries and of those who knew him best. I suspect that Izaak Walton and Edward Hyde (Clarendon) put down in their famous portraits more than their own judgments. Some of Hyde's portraits sound like the summing up of the combined opinion of a picked jury of contemporaries.

and entertaining man he was and we all liked him, but a lazy beggar he was at all times who never put matters to the touch. He was at his best in a tavern with three or four friends, full of high spirits and sly sayings, but a shy one with those he did not know well, or in any large company. You have missed much else, his courtly manners with the few women he liked, and his way of avoiding other women.

Dudley Carleton knew even more about him than Sir Rowland and could perhaps have penetrated further into hidden matters. If I could have had a long gossip with him he might have unbent and have told me what he thought of his long-time friend. Would he have declared that Chamberlain was at heart a disappointed man who knew himself quite as able as many whose careers he watched, but that he was essentially easy-going and timid, afraid to enter the competition for power and place? To withdraw from the race at the beginning and to assume the attitude of an observer was easy and became at length natural. Carleton, had he said so much, would have put it less analytically and more in metaphors.

Winwood knew Chamberlain, who was always making inquiries about the chances of his protégé and seeking in every way to further Carleton's career. Winwood and Chamberlain had spent long evenings together over the dinner-table at Ditton, and Winwood, had he forgotten himself for the time being, could conceivably have given us much light upon the man in whom we are interested.

I am afraid that the comments of Sir Rowland, of Sir Dudley, and of Sir Ralph would have left me crestfallen. So much they might have told me that I could never have guessed. Yet it is possible that the historian can by a close study of many letters learn aspects of a man's character hidden from his contemporaries.

Chamberlain's friendships shifted gradually, as do those of

most people, partly because of his growing disinclination to travel far enough to visit them, partly because his friends were growing feeble or dying, partly because some of them, agreeable enough in youth, seemed tedious in old age. In 1615 he wrote to Carleton that he loved no straggling journeys and that travelling by horse had become wearisome to him, so that for three years he had not been to visit the Michael Dormers, nor the Borlases, nor the Backhouses. The Dormers came in that year to London to consult their physician; Lady Dormer died in 1616 and Sir Michael lingered on a few years stricken with paralysis. As for Sir Edward Norris, whom Chamberlain had often visited in earlier years, Chamberlain confessed to Carleton that he should not mind if he took his farewell of him. Sir Edward had grown pompous and was inclined to be patronizing. The Wallops in some way dropped out of Chamberlain's letters, although occasionally Chamberlain ran into them in London. The merriest of his friends, Sir Rowland Lytton, declined into dotage, and Chamberlain was relieved at his death in 1615. He had long feared that Sir Rowland would outlive himself.

It seemed indeed that 1615 marked a kind of 'climacteric' with Chamberlain's friends. Sir Ralph Winwood and Sir Henry Fanshawe were still alive, however, and Chamberlain, in spite of a growing aversion to visiting, continued to stay at Ditton and at Ware Park. Both men died in 1616.

His friends were dropping out and the pageant of events was less spectacular. He had lived much of his life in Elizabethan days and things were not as when the time had been. No longer did ships lie in wait for Spanish carracks laden with treasure. On the contrary, when the Princess Elizabeth had to cross the Channel to join her husband, the Elector Palatine, all shipping had to be held in port lest there should be wanting the 2500 sailors necessary to man the ships that were to accompany her.

Even crime had become less dramatic. When a noble adventurer had moved to seize the Elizabethan Government he had tried to do it in the grand manner. But less than twenty years after the failure of Essex, Chamberlain counted eight former Councillors in the Tower confined there for displeasing the King, or for mishandling funds, or merely for murder. About the murder there was little drama; a great and beautiful lady had resorted to slow poisoning. The grand manner had gone out with the great Queen.

VI

For the Crown Chamberlain had that reverence to be expected from a man of that time. That reverence is expressed again and again by the characters in Shakespeare. Yet Chamberlain knew as well as Shakespeare that kings were but men and were not always wise and good. It did not take him long to detect the weaknesses of James I but he was too canny to state them baldly in his letters. He was content to relate episodes and allow Carleton to draw his own conclusions. His stories of the Court, when added together, afford us more clues as to the character of James I than any other source; incidentally they tell us much of Chamberlain's standards of judgment. His codes of conduct and behaviour were those of the moderate Englishmen of that gentle class who had most to say.

That James was a vain and self-important man was soon evident to his more knowing subjects, and especially to members of Parliament who had to listen to his many and long-winded pronouncements in which he was constantly comparing himself to the godhead. His intense egoism crept out in every fourth sentence. Chamberlain never used that word of course; it had not yet come into use. He merely allowed James to show off. The King declared that he never affected anything much and seriously but it came to good pass. When some of the courtiers told the Sovereign that it was not the fashion to have a play on Christmas night James replied: 'I will make it a fashion', possibly the earliest attribution of that boast to a crowned head. One evening the King was dining in greater state than usual and Chamberlain could not understand why until he reflected that some Scottish visitors were looking on, and that James wished them to see him in all his glory, and to carry back to the north an account of his splendour.

The bad manners of James were the sport of Anthony Weldon, who disliked Scots and despised the King. His picture of the strutting Sovereign was used by Sir Walter Scott in his *Fortunes of Nigel*. Nowhere does Chamberlain suggest such a gauche figure as Weldon and others describe; he had too much respect for the royal personage. He does, however, manage to indicate that the King was not always the personification of graciousness. James had been up most of two nights and was on the third night watching the masque and showing signs of boredom when Sir Francis Bacon, quick to sense the situation, explained to the Sovereign that by the disgrace of his want of interest the masquers would be quickly buried. James replied that they must bury him quickly, for he could not last much longer. Then he remembered his duty and with a graciousness he could at times command listened to the performance. On another occasion, however, he was less considerate. The Bishop of London was preaching and appears to have been uttering opinions not acceptable to the royal authority on theology. The King grew so loud that the Bishop was forced to close his sermon abruptly.

The emotionalism of the King, Chamberlain noted without comment. When Prince Charles and the Duke of Buckingham returned from their madcap journey to Spain the King was as usual hunting in the vicinity of Royston, north of London. Chamberlain records that the Prince and the favourite, as soon as they reached London, proceeded to the hunting centre. Down the stairs rushed the King to meet them, 'where the Prince and the Duke being on their knees the King fell on their necks and they all wept'.

The King was given to over-intimacy. In personal affairs he had a Scot's interest and was never loath to take advantage of his position. When a good-looking young woman, as Chamberlain tells the story, was saying goodbye to the Court on her return to her home in France, the King banteringly urged her to stay on in England, suggesting various English matches for her and promising that whomsoever she would marry he would make an earl. The morning after the King's daughter, Elizabeth, had been wedded to Frederick, the Elector Palatine, nothing would do but the King must visit the 'young turtles' and strictly examine the Prince as to whether he was his true son-in-law, and was sufficiently assured, says Chamberlain dryly.

Chamberlain thought the King officious. Men and women were thrown into the Tower for foolish words and for indiscretions that might well have been overlooked. It is probable that Chamberlain reflected some public opinion when he remarked:

> I should rather wish him to contemn these barking whelps and all their bawlings than to trouble himself with them, and bring these things to scanning, for it breeds but more speech, and to see silly men so severely censured begets commiseration.

What worried Chamberlain more was the way in which the King threw money around. He was constantly bestowing thousands of pounds in Crown lands or in other revenues upon his favourites and their friends. It is impossible to estimate the amount he gave to Buckingham and his relatives. It was believed at the time that James Hay, the Scot, who became Viscount Doncaster and eventually Earl of Carlisle, received in all something like £400,000 from royal bounty. At a time when the Government was so pressed for money that it could not pay its officials and when ambassadors were begging for back pay or at least for their official expenses, James was proposing, wrote Chamberlain, to give £10,000 in jewels to the evil woman who was to become Countess of Somerset.

Chamberlain never said so in so many words but he made it clear enough that he did not regard the King as a good judge of men.[1] He would probably have made an exception of Robert Cecil, who was a carry-over from the days of Elizabeth and who would have seemed to Chamberlain an English gentleman of the old school. His friends depended so much upon the favour of Cecil that he would have been reticent in making any judgment. But it is doubtful if any other members of the inner circle around James were regarded by Chamberlain as suitable leaders of England. After the death of Cecil in 1612 James fell much under the influence of the two Howards – Thomas, Earl of Suffolk, and Henry, Earl of Northampton. It is easy to read between the lines that Chamberlain admired none of the Howard family. As for the favourites, Robert Carr and after him George Villiers, Chamberlain said little, but quite enough for us to see that they were not among his heroes. At one time he remarked: 'Many times unfitness and unlikeliness make a thing seem more likely.' He was thinking at the time of possible appointments ahead and no doubt was really thinking of what usually happened. He did not admire those whom the King chose to honour but he was an Englishman and always prepared to accept the realities of the situation.

To Chamberlain the King seemed indecisive. As a young ruler in Scotland he had shown resolution but in England he changed

[1] So far as his favourites allowed him to do so James made use of Sir George Calvert, of Sir Julius Caesar, and of Sir Ralph Winwood, all of whom had been in the Civil Service and were competent at their jobs. Moreover he pushed Lionel Cranfield, who understood finances, and tried, although rather weakly, to stand by him when Buckingham turned against him. John Williams was an effective administrator but Buckingham found him in his way.

his course too often. He would become excited over a certain foreign policy and then, when vigorous action was called for, draw in his horns. In discussing the Amboyna massacre by the Dutch, Chamberlain remarked:

> The King takes it so to heart that he speaks somewhat exuberantly and I could wish he would say less so he would do more.

In dealing with the House of Commons James was equally vacillating. He would threaten them and then three days later would talk graciously to them and presently would revert to threats. In making appointments to posts in the Government he changed his course in midstream. Chamberlain wrote:

> There is scant any resolution firm here but that it may alter once in four and twenty hours.

To Chamberlain the King seemed to be sitting in the midst of a world of intrigue, playing men off one against another. That game James liked to call kingcraft and believed himself an old hand at it. 'He forgets not business,' wrote Chamberlain, 'but he hath found the art of frustrating men's expectations and holding them in suspense.' It was his pleasure to send for a man who aspired to a vacant office and to make such a fuss over him that the man thought himself as good as appointed and accepted the felicitations of his friends. Then suddenly James would drop him and show like attentions to someone else. Such shifts provided drama for the Court but indicated a vein of cruelty. For the men so 'sucked and drawn dry' by the King, Chamberlain could not conceal his pity.

As the King grew old he lost interest even in the game of keeping men on the griddle. 'That vigour', wrote Chamberlain, 'begins to relent and he must daily more and more intend his own health and quiet.' To judge from Chamberlain's descriptions and from other contemporary accounts the hunting field was more and more occupying his attention. The filling of offices he turned over to George Villiers, Marquis and later Duke of Buckingham, who was by no means loath to accept the responsibility. James was off to Royston and to Newmarket. Once some years earlier when the hard-working Cecil, whom James dubbed his 'little beagle', was ill the King came to see him and told him, with unusual graciousness, that if he should ever fail 'there were no more safe hunting for the King of England'. When he was too weak or ill to hunt he would settle indoors, Chamberlain tells us, 'till he had his deer brought to make a muster before him'. The spectacle of a weary old sovereign asking to have the deer driven before him would have interested Shakespeare. Men found it hard to keep the King indoors. 'He is so desirous to see certain hawks fly, that he would not be stayed.'

Historians have been reluctant to say much about the inclination of James to surround himself with good-looking young men. Robert Carr became a favourite, Earl of Somerset and a power in the land, by virtue of one qualification, his good looks, and the story of George Villiers was much the same. So well did the Court understand the weakness of the King that those who hoped to bring about a change of power would introduce handsome young men into the royal presence in an effort to displace Robert Carr and then Villiers, 'the principal verb', as Chamberlain puts it tersely. Never once does our letter-writer suggest that the weakness of James was unnatural; so careful was he to say nothing of the sort that he leaves us curious. It is hard in the literature of the time to find allusions to the matter, except in a cipher diary where we learn that the students of Gray's Inn were less reticent.

On the other hand James could be a trifle soft about good-looking young women. At one time he was so taken up with three comely sisters that he extolled them before all others and bespoke them for the Court against the next Christmas. Yet he grew tired of the intrigues of women about the Court. When he was ready to name George Calvert as Secretary he had him in and quizzed him about his wife. Calvert was able to assure James of her goodness and discretion. Not all could be so recommended. The King, wrote Chamberlain, was in a great vein of taking down high-handed women. He found support from the clergy, usually anxious to please. The Bishop of London called the clergy of his diocese together and told them expressly that they should inveigh in their sermons against the insolency of women and should denounce the wearing by them of broad-brimmed hats, pointed doublets and short hair. The clergy were obedient; the Dean of Westminster would not allow women with yellow ruffs to be admitted to pews.

That was going too far. James heard from some of the women. He relented a bit, as often, and put a gloss on his words, saying that his meaning was not for yellow ruffs but for other manlike and unseemly attire. Meanwhile, however, the pulpits were ringing with the insolence of women and Chamberlain noted that the players and ballad-makers were taking up the theme. It was what the English today would call silly-season stuff.

It would appear that women were playing a larger role in affairs than ever before. The great ladies at Court were more important than they had ever been in English history. All the masques and balls which at holiday seasons followed one another night after night, all the fine doings of an extravagant and ostentatious society which Chamberlain records, had accentuated the role of women. John Milton had been a boy in those times but he had no doubt listened to his elders talking and was possibly thinking of the Jacobean Court when he wrote:

> Store of ladies whose bright eyes
> Rain influence and judge the prize.

For the effeminate society that grew up James was of course much to blame. Where a favourite ruled and with the assistance of his mother[1] matched his nieces and cousins to men who hoped to get on, and where other great ladies were able to gain great financial favours for themselves and their friends, the King had to expect that women would vaunt their power.

In general, Chamberlain by his stories indicated again and again James's want of kingliness.[2] There was a want of royal dignity in the King's choice of interests. His predecessor had been interested in personalities, even in the petty spites of ladies-in-waiting, but had kept the best of her mind for significant issues. There was a want of majesty in the royal person. One has only to look at the portraits of James I in the National Gallery, at Hatfield and at Hampton Court to realize that lack of breeding which Chamberlain and his friends must always have felt as they heard of his behaviour. Indeed there was something ridiculous about him. Even his clothes were not well set upon him. Those in a quiet corner must have found it hard to resist laughing at his high and mighty manner, but it was not healthy even to smile about such things. That James had a Scottish burr would have made it easier to mock him, had anyone even in small groups dared to do so. No one told all the truth about the King's unmajestical ways until long after his death but Chamberlain's letters offered many clues.

[1] Buckingham's mother was said to have started her career as Mary Beaumont, a gentlewoman on the staff of Brooksby Hall, Leicestershire. Sir George Villiers observed her figure and had her wait on his wife, and when his wife died, married her. She became the mother of George Villiers and is said to have trained him for a place at Court. As young George rose through favour to his dukedom he did not forget his mother and she did not forget her two other sons, who were both ennobled. Eventually she was created Countess of Buckingham and became a power at Court. She undoubtedly had brains and was the ancestor of many of the great in the British aristocracy.

[2] For two sorts of person, a contemporary wrote, James never had a kindness, 'those whose hawks and dogs ran as well as his own, and those who were able to speak as much reason as himself'. His capacity for absorbing flattery can hardly be overestimated. When it was not forthcoming he would praise himself, as in his addresses to Parliament, and almost purr with satisfaction over his own words. Yet he could recognize talent and even welcome good ideas.

The truth is that Chamberlain had never been impressed by the King, even at the beginning of his reign when everyone was praising James's learning and wisdom. Chamberlain said little good about him at any time and understood his weaknesses as well as any contemporary who left a record. He was as just to him as any Englishman with English traditions and the memory before him of the great Queen could have been. He was not easily tolerant of foreigners, nor of the self-important, nor of those who were noisy or over-intimate.

His attitude towards Prince Charles was different. The Prince was beginning, he noted, to frequent the meetings of the House of Lords and his affability and courtesy there were winning him goodwill. He could not in a whole age have lighted on such a school to learn experience and to try diversity of wits and humours. The character of the Prince pleased him as being free from any vicious and scandalous inclinations. He was grown a fine gentleman beyond any expectation Chamberlain had of him. No doubt Chamberlain remembered that as a child Charles had been deemed very backward.

VII

Chamberlain's letters have many allusions to the famous jurist, Sir Edward Coke, and more to his second wife. Coke had legal learning and a capacity for close reasoning, a wife from the Norfolk Pastons with £30,000, and the backing of William Cecil, the great Elizabethan Lord Burghley, to aid him in getting on. When his wife died he married within a few months Lady Hatton, the widowed daughter of Thomas Cecil, Earl of Exeter, and thus a granddaughter of Coke's early patron, and a niece of Sir Robert Cecil. That Lady Hatton had been courted by Francis Bacon, his rival at Court, made Coke's conquest the sweeter. Chamberlain expressed surprise that Lady Hatton should decline to a man of Coke's quality and hinted at some mystery about it. Why a mystery? Lady Hatton was a Cecil, a figure at Court, and endowed with Dorset acres, but Sir Edward was a rising young lawyer, with colour and force of personality, with features that did not lessen his appeal to the female sex, and with an assurance that is seldom a handicap.

His progress during the reign of Elizabeth had been as rapid as could have been expected by a young man on his way. With the new sovereign he was bound sooner or later to come into conflict. James had an itch for instructing, and the judges offered him an opportunity. To him the duty of a judge was to assist the Crown against those who would diminish its authority, to support royal power against the forces of disorder. James remembered the anarchic history of Scotland and the need there for strong government. Sir Edward looked back on another kind of history, that of England, where the power of the sovereign had been slowly limited by precedent and legal decisions. To him the function of a judge was to render decisions between king and subject, and in doing so, he must be free from pressure. Like many another, Coke exalted the power of his own profession and was able to find in the law some reinforcement of his own importance. He was obstinate enough, once he had taken a stand, to sacrifice his own career for so good a cause. He could not be conciliatory.

James had to put up with a good deal from the judge; from his own point of view he was rather long-suffering with him. But at length he dropped him from the Privy Council and removed him from the Chief Justiceship of the Common Pleas to that of the King's Bench, a post in which he would be less able to thwart the Crown.

With Coke's resistance to the King Chamberlain did not show

himself sympathetic; rather he seemed concerned that Coke was falling behind in the race for position and power, a race in which he was always interested, for other people. He did imply that Coke's fall from favour was not a real disgrace.

For all his Gray's Inn experience Chamberlain was not worried about royal encroachments on the law, as were many of the barristers. He looked less at principles than at personalities. People said, he wrote, that Coke had been 'too busy in the late business . . . and dived further into secrets than there was need'. By the late business Chamberlain meant the trial of the Earl and Countess of Somerset for the murder of Overbury, an episode I shall mention later.

What interested Chamberlain more about Coke was his difficulties with his second wife. The great Lady Hatton had devoted her first years as Coke's wife to forwarding her husband's fortunes. But she was an outspoken woman, as opinionated and self-willed as her husband. Although she made enemies at Court, not the least of whom was Queen Anne, she remained a power there, so much so that men on the make would seek her favour. She had her 'mignons', or pet young men, and when promotions were going, would further their interests in every way she could.

It was more than she did for her husband, after the first few years. As soon as he fell into disgrace she

> divided herself from him and disfurnished his house in Holborn and at Stoke [Poges] of whatsoever was in them, and carried all the movables and plate she could come by God knows whither.

The property differences of the couple were brought before the Privy Council and Lady Coke appeared there, accompanied by Cecils and Howards, and 'declaimed bitterly against him [her husband] and so carried herself that divers said Burbage could not have acted better'.

The quarrel between husband and wife grew more bitter over the disposition of the younger daughter, who was only fourteen, but a considerable heiress. The Villiers family, never averse to alliances with property, proposed to endow the favourite's elder brother, Sir John, who had little to recommend him either in mind or body, by marrying him to Frances Coke. Sir Edward was asked to put up £10,000 for the marriage, but would promise only two-thirds of that sum. After delays he was persuaded to agree to the marriage. To antagonize the Villiers family was looking for trouble.

Lady Coke set herself against the marriage. That Sir John, apart from his relationship, was not a desirable husband, may have been the reason for her opposition. At any rate she carried off her daughter to the house of a friend. Coke secured a warrant from Secretary Winwood, went to the house where his daughter was, broke open the doors, and abducted his daughter. In spite of pursuit by the mother, he was able to deposit his daughter with Lady Compton, Villiers's mother. The episode, wrote Chamberlain, 'hath furnished Paul's and this town very plentifully for a whole week'.

Frances was married to Sir John. It was not long before Chamberlain wrote:

> The young Lady Villiers is sent to her aunt . . . some say upon discontent, others more likely that the humour in Sir John Villiers' leg bursts forth again, so that her company might do him harm: howsoever it is, he is accounted but a weak man and not long-lived, so that there needed not so much ado to get him a wife.

Sir John was presently created Viscount Purbeck, his title coming from his wife's lands in Dorset, but a peerage produced no improvement either in his wits or in his health. Lady Purbeck took on at length a lover, and was in and out of church courts for adultery. What seemed to the public a high-comedy situation became for Lady Purbeck a tragedy. Coke had sacrificed his daughter to his ambition.

The sacrifice proved of little value. Coke was restored to the Privy Council but never regained the favour of the King or of Buckingham. He became at length a spokesman of the opposition to the King in the House of Commons. That stage in Coke's career did not interest Chamberlain so much, but he wrote that Coke 'continues still the bellwether and leads the flock' in the Commons. To the average man, even to the average member of the House of Commons, Sir Edward seemed to be the leader, because he spoke with force and liveliness and had the character to make his every word seem impressive. He was full of learning and pat stories and most members did not realize that his memory was often at fault and that the precedents he cited were sometimes less apposite than they seemed. He led the Commons down one or two by-paths and drew them into a maze from which the real leaders of the Commons had to extricate them. Never a very wise man, he was in the estimation of the public the grand old man of Westminster. Of Coke's failure in Parliament Chamberlain was not aware, so far as we know.

VIII

Coke's rival from the later days of Elizabeth on was Sir Francis Bacon, who was the son of an Elizabethan Lord Keeper and on his mother's side a cousin of Robert Cecil.[1] Bacon had made his mark in late Elizabethan parliaments and had been a protégé of that Earl of Essex whom Elizabeth had long favoured and whom she finally had to send to the block. Bacon must have talked to Chamberlain more than once, for they had at least four acquaintances in common, two of whom were close friends of Chamberlain: Carleton, Bodley, Lancelot Andrewes and Toby Matthews.

[1] His mother was one of the five remarkable daughters of Sir Anthony Cooke.

Chamberlain records no meeting with Bacon until after Bacon had become Lord Chancellor, when Chamberlain was asked to dine with him and was treated with kindness and familiarity.

It was not indeed until Bacon became Solicitor General in 1607 that he began to appear frequently in the letters of Chamberlain, who was not likely to overlook a rising young man. Between the lines of those letters it is easy to read that Chamberlain was not drawn to him. Probably the Paul's-walker, like many others, could not quite forget that Bacon, after having been closely associated with the Earl of Essex, had at the time of his brief rebellion turned sharply against that impetuous man and had assisted in developing the case against him. A certain loyalty to old friends and patrons was regarded as decorous. In any case Chamberlain, who was fond of the give-and-take of friendly people, would not have been drawn to a man who was almost pure intellect and who had little interest in others except as useful pawns.

From the place of Solicitor-General, Bacon was advanced to that of Attorney-General. There was apprehension, Chamberlain reported, that he might prove a 'dangerous instrument'. In the first years of the reign of James I Bacon had again and again been the honest broker between Sovereign and Parliament, advising James how to hold the loyalty of the members and suggesting to the Commons how to put their case in such a way as to conciliate the King. But as he became a power in the Government and hoped through influence with the Crown to mould state policy to his heart's desire, he tended to exalt the royal prerogative. 'The world', wrote Chamberlain, 'begins already to complain of some incroaching courses and say if things should thus proceed, men's estates would be in danger.'[1] Bacon was in favour with the King, as Chamberlain perceived, and was ready to comply with the wishes of the King or with those of his favourite.

[1] The King could withdraw Crown property long leased on easy terms from the holders in order to bestow it on his friends. Furthermore his forced loans might be carried very far.

His compliance was again and again evident. When Coke stood out in the case of Prohibitions and in the Commendam Case and in other cases for the independence of the judges against the Crown's interference with their decisions, Bacon was on the side of the King and eager to entrap Coke. Coke was required to present a list of errors in his work. 'The worst is', wrote Chamberlain, 'that the Lord Chancellor, the Attorney [Bacon], and the Solicitor prosecute him implacably.' Nothing pleased Bacon more than to catch out his old rival. He had already written to the King accusing Coke of 'innovations', and offering reasons why Coke should not be made Lord Chancellor. For that great post Bacon had another candidate.

Bacon was scoring heavily against Coke and strengthening his position with the King. When Robert Carr, the royal favourite, married Frances Howard, who had wriggled free from her husband, the Earl of Essex, Bacon gave a masque in honour of the couple at the cost of £2000. When the scene changed and Carr and his wife were accused of the murder of Overbury, it became the duty of Bacon as Attorney-General to take a leading part in the prosecution. He was able quickly to attach himself to the new favourite, George Villiers, and was made a Privy Councillor.

In 1617 he became Lord Keeper and rode in triumph to Westminster 'accompanied by most of the Council and nobility about this town, with other gallants to the number of more than 200 horse, besides the judges and Inns of Court'. Chamberlain was told, probably by lawyer friends, that Bacon was no great man of law. He reported also that a woman had been heard telling the King that Bacon was no keeper, alluding no doubt to his extravagant ways.

He had long lived beyond his means.[1] Eight years before

[1] James is said to have remarked of Bacon: 'He and I shall both die beggars.' Fuller, *Church History*, V, 497-98.

the dénouement of the Bacon tragedy Chamberlain wrote:

> He carries a great port as well in his train as in his apparel and other ways, and lives at a great charge, and yet he pretends he will take no fees nor intermeddle in mercenary causes.

Bacon's publications did not escape Chamberlain's attention. When the *Instauratio Magna* appeared, a Paul's-walker commented that a fool could not have written such a book and a wise man would not, while others chuckled over the remark attributed to James that the book was like the peace of God that passeth understanding. *The History of the Reign of King Henry the Seventh* won Chamberlain's admiration. What a pity it was, he wrote, that the author of such a masterpiece should ever have other employment.[1] In other words Chamberlain did not believe that Bacon was fitted for high office. Had he been on the scene in another and more propitious time, however, had he been cast in a slightly different mould, he might have proved as imaginative a statesman as he was a thinker.

He missed statesmanship but he became in 1617 Lord Chancellor, the post to which his rival might have aspired. As Chancellor he continued to study to please. The aldermen of London were planning to elect a Recorder of their own choosing but the new Chancellor interfered to suggest a nominee acceptable to the King and to Buckingham.

He did not escape criticism. An Oxford man, Singleton, a canon of St. Paul's declaimed bitterly against his court (i.e. the Chancery) and 'glanced (they say) somewhat scandalously at him and his Catamites, as he called them'. Bacon had Singleton committed. He was riding so high that he might well have ignored the canon.

[1] Bacon had once written to Sir Thomas Bodley of himself as 'fitter to hold a book than to play a part'. *Cabala* (1691), p. 66.

Then suddenly out of what seemed sunny skies came lightning and thunder. Bacon was accused in a committee of the House of Commons of accepting bribes as a judge, and the charges were supported by witnesses. As soon as his position was jeopardized new witnesses came forward against him. The Commons could not hope to move successfully against the favourite, the Duke of Buckingham, but they could proceed against the Lord Chancellor who had been his instrument and a supporter of the royal prerogative. It is altogether possible that Buckingham was willing to see Bacon thrown to the wolves. Chamberlain expressed regret that a man of such excellent parts should prove so foul and faulty as was alleged, but he did not seem surprised. He was seldom surprised at the weaknesses of men and he had clearly been aware of Bacon's failing. What did amaze him was that the late Lord Chancellor had so little realization of his own disgrace and that he continued to be as vain and idle in all his humours as when he was at his highest. Of what had happened to him Bacon was indeed more aware than he pretended, but he hoped that some turn of the wheel might bring him to the top again. Had not the King forgiven men for sins worse than accepting bribes? The Viscount of St. Albans, as he had become shortly before his fall, never gave up hope, subjecting himself during the rest of his life to unnecessary snubs.[1]

Unlike many of his generation Chamberlain gained no satisfaction from seeing the mighty brought low. He had tears for human suffering and, while recognizing that Bacon was to blame, was genuinely sorry for him. The excuse put forward for that great mind that he was only following the practice of the time Chamberlain did not bring up. No one knew better than Cham-

[1] There is a pitiful letter from Bacon in which he urges Buckingham to use him quietly about great matters, and adds: 'To hear the wind and not to feel it will make one sleep the better.' Goodman, II, 234. William Sanderson (*Aulicus Coquinarie*, p. 174) tells us how Prince Charles espied Bacon after his disgrace accompanied by a goodly troop of horsemen and remarked: 'This man scorns to go out like a snuff.'

berlain how many lordly mansions had been built in his time from money accepted for political favours. Possibly he felt that the position of a judge demanded greater honesty than that of other officials. Perhaps the sin seemed the greater from the public disgrace.

IX

With Sir Thomas Bodley Chamberlain had been long acquainted. Bodley was a stepfather of Lady Winwood, the wife of one of Chamberlain's intimates, as we have seen. In his later years Bodley became a man of one idea, to create a library at Oxford University. He persuaded the Stationers' Office to bestow one copy of every book published in England upon the new library. He interested Sir John Bennet, who had to do with the probate of wills, in obtaining from legacies left to pious uses money for the library. He besought his friends for books for the library. It was natural that he received praise from the University of Oxford and that praise he was not reticent in relaying to his friends.

Chamberlain had never esteemed Bodley highly but he had a marginal liking for him as for one who had been a part of his experience. He was sorry to hear of Bodley's increasing illness. Sir Thomas was calling in various physicians and was by no means ready to accept their unfavourable verdict. It is easier for friends than for the victim to be reconciled to bad news. At length Chamberlain reported Sir Thomas as speechless and about to die. 'God comfort him and send him a good passage.'

Bodley's death did not waken in his friends a new realization of his virtues. On the contrary he set him down as having been drunk with the applause and vanity of his library. The verses and orations that the University had heaped upon him would soon, Chamberlain predicted, be used to stop mustard pots. The will Sir Thomas left did nothing to better Chamberlain's judgment of him. Seven thousand pounds Bodley bestowed on the library at Oxford but left his stepchildren, including Lady Winwood, with but little. Those stepchildren were the offspring of the wealthy widow whom Bodley had married, and the money, Chamberlain asserted, had been largely hers.[1]

Nor was it heart-warming to his friends that Bodley in his distribution of post-mortem presents preferred to leave tokens to those great people whom he had happened to know and left out his less important associates. It was seldom that Chamberlain betrayed sensitiveness to slights but he was obviously a little hurt that Sir Thomas had failed to leave him any memento. He was not surprised to learn that Bodley had left behind him a seven-sheet account of his life, mentioning every honour received but saying nothing about his wife or about Walsingham and Leicester, 'who were all his main raisers'.

Bodley is still honoured and Bodley's library, the Bodleian, is one of the best in the world and a place where scholars delight to go. Chamberlain has been abused for having spoken as he did of so great a benefactor of learning. No plan for gaining immortality is likely to be more successful than was that of Bodley.

A pleasanter figure in Chamberlain's letters to Carleton is an old friend of both men, Sir Ralph Winwood. Like Carleton he had been a diplomat, moving from one post to another and cherishing the unconquerable hope of eventual service at home close to the throne. In such a career-man Chamberlain was naturally interested and he had known him a long time. Now and then he wrote him the same type of newsy epistle he sent to

[1] Frances Troup ('Biography of John Bodley, the father of Sir Thomas Bodley', *Devon. Trans.* XXXV, 167-97) takes no stock in the theory that Sir Thomas obtained his fortune from his widow and failed to leave her children the property due them. Cf. an earlier article about John Bodley in *Devon. Trans.* VIII, 554-5, from *Notes and Queries.* John More, writing to Winwood in January and February 1613, took the same view of Bodley's conduct to his stepchildren as Chamberlain. See Buccleuch MSS., I, 124 et seq.

Carleton; indeed the letters were sometimes almost duplicates of those posted to Carleton.

Winwood's career had in it that element of suspense agreeable to a news-gatherer. He was often mentioned, after the death of Cecil in 1612, for the office of Secretary, and for two years Chamberlain's letters were concerned off and on with the ups and downs of Winwood's chances. Chamberlain would be hopeful and then discouraged. 'I learned a song when I was a little one (which I cannot forget) that blessed is the wooing that is not long a-doing.' The delay in the naming of a Secretary frequently cast him down. But the wooing was at length successful and in March 1614, 'after many traverses', Winwood was sworn Principal Secretary.

For Chamberlain there followed three happy years. He saw the Winwoods in town and at their country house at Ditton. That place they brought to a good pass with a new dove house, a paved court, a conduit of water and fine ponds. They had filled up the moat, planted a large orchard, made spacious gardens with delicate arbours and a fair brick wall around it, and had furnished the house 'without any great cost or curiosity'. It was largely Lady Winwood's doing and Chamberlain approved of all her actions. She had busied herself among flowers and plants and took pleasure in setting and tending melons, a skill she may have learned in the Low Countries. She loved fruit as well as any woman he knew.

Chamberlain was likely to be at Winwood's town house or country house whenever that statesman was given any leisure by the King. He was used with such extraordinary favour and familiarity that he could not but be gratified. Between the lines of his letters to Carleton one can read that much of the information he was forwarding was coming from Winwood.[1]

[1] Winwood (February 24th, 1614. S.P. 14/76, No. 34) writing to my Lord —— (presumably Carleton) mentioned their mutual friend Chamberlain 'whom I do freely communicate all I know of worth and importance'.

Chamberlain was able to be of service to his friend abroad. Carleton had ventured to write Winwood a frank letter of advice about his policy and Chamberlain found the Secretary angry about the letter and certain that it had been circulated to others, as many letters were, and that Chamberlain had seen it. When Chamberlain assured him that he had not seen it Winwood appeared mollified. But Chamberlain felt it necessary to tell Carleton that it was a tickle point to offer advice to one sure of himself.

Winwood was, Chamberlain feared, too sure of himself. It was unnecessary for him to be so loyal to Sir Edward Coke. Coke, as we have seen, was being pressed by the King and was obviously in growing disfavour. Chamberlain wished Winwood would not presume so much on the strength of his own shoulders as to think that he alone could bear up the ruins of a building that was falling. 'He hath more courage than needs', wrote the cautious Chamberlain. On another occasion he noted that Winwood was so confident that there was no advising him. That was hard luck for Chamberlain who enjoyed an advisory capacity. It did not occur to Chamberlain that the confidence Winwood exhibited might prove an element of strength with a weak and indolent King. The trouble was, and of course Chamberlain realized as much, that there was a second king, George Villiers, and no one could guess just how long Villiers would put up with such a masterful man as Winwood. 'The pitcher goes so long to the water that at last it comes broken home', wrote Chamberlain to Carleton. In certain matters he hoped that Winwood would not meddle.

Within three weeks Chamberlain had to report the death of Winwood after an illness of only a few days:

> You may think what a loss I have of so good a friend now in my latter age when I have most need of comfort, and

> indeed it was a kind of new life to me to see his kindness increase daily towards me and that we still grew nearer.

Chamberlain took his loss as well as he could but his letters were never so cheerful again. He continued to visit Lady Winwood at Ditton.

X

Sir Henry Wotton, whose letters[1] and poetry have made him something of a literary figure, interested Chamberlain a great deal because he was another career-man, though a less successful one. Chamberlain did not like him but he heard about him all the time and could not but observe his comings and goings. Sir Henry was three times ambassador to Venice, carried out other diplomatic missions for James, and was in and out of Court, always seeking advancement.

His career had started hopefully. He had been of use to James when James was ruler of Scotland and was remembered gratefully by that Sovereign when he became King of England.[2] He was believed to be in the good books of Cecil and was in favour with Prince Henry and with Queen Anne. The death of Salisbury (Cecil) and of Prince Henry left him less befriended at Court but he was not easily discouraged. It was Chamberlain's opinion that Wotton insinuated himself by the most unworthy means, though he does not tell us how. Of his behaviour Chamberlain wrote:

> Fabritio [Wotton] gives himself *buon tempo* and follows good company and plays as familiarly and ordinarily as if he had nothing else to do.

[1] *The Life and Letters of Sir Henry Wotton*, ed. Logan Pearsall Smith, (Oxford, 2 vols., 1907).

[2] A long and interesting story, too long to be told here.

A little later Chamberlain reported that Wotton was 'down the wind and his business begins to quail'.

Wotton had himself to blame. Given to jokes, he made one too many. In a guest-room of a German inn he had written down that an ambassador was an honest man who was sent to lie abroad for the good of his country, and the jest had been brought to the ears of the King. Wotton explained that his inscription had been a merriment, but James, who enjoyed no jokes but his own, thought it no laughing matter.

It took Wotton a long while to ingratiate himself again even a little with the King but he did not want persistence. 'Signor Fabritio is never from him [the King], indeed it is all the work he hath to do.' He was full of diplomatic projects. He would marry Prince Charles to the Princess of Savoy. 'He takes upon him to propound many new devices, and would fain be a director where there is no need of his help.'

A secretaryship he hoped for, but he accepted gladly a mission to negotiate with the Dutch about Cleves, 'so that you may see that his stomach is come down'. The English captains at The Hague reported that he was ever busy and dispatching little.

Sir Henry was at length sent to Venice again, to succeed Carleton there, but went away from London as slowly as possible, still hoping, Chamberlain implied, for something better. In Venice he was unhappy. While others were prospering at home he thought of himself as 'gathering of cockles upon this lake, impatient more of the shame than of the sense of want'. He had bored the King who was glad to have him 'least in sight'.

Eventually he was let down with the provostship of Eton and a pension from the King. There he entertained guests, made a fuss over the boys, and became a figure in the history of the school.

To Chamberlain Wotton was evidently a kind of Polonius, given to wise saws and continental instances, an ambitious little man destined to remain unsatisfied. There had been something undignified in his pursuit of office,[1] and Chamberlain valued dignity in all things, and success.

Chamberlain was less than fair to him. Wotton was perhaps too Europeanized to meet the approval of a Londoner born and bred. Yet Wotton was very English; English, let us say, of the mid-nineteenth century. He was really devoted to his country, thinking always of her position in the world; he hoped to see her leading Europe as the head and front of Protestantism.[2] He was full of moral indignation and yet, like many of the righteous, could turn sharp corners. Unlike Chamberlain he had to make a living; diplomacy was his craft, and holding office his means of support. He was not a bore, as Chamberlain implies, though no doubt he wearied those who suffered from his importunities.[3] He could talk wisely and wittily. That he was not always effective and had foolish schemes and overplayed his hand is likely enough. Words were his medium and he was essentially an amateur. What he did best was to write letters, a talent Chamberlain should have valued, but he had little chance to see the letters.[4] Chamberlain had pity even for failures, but that pity was reserved for those whom he liked.

Wotton was not only a good letter-writer – not as good as Chamberlain – but a poet. We cannot but be sorry for him as we read again his most famous poem, 'The Character of Happy Life':

> How happy is he born and taught
> That serveth not another's will.

[1] Wotton thought of himself as condemned by an unfortunate bashfulness in his own business, that is, that he was not pushing enough. *Cabala* (1691), p. 367.

[2] Aubrey says that Milton was a good friend of Wotton, 'who delighted in his company'. Aubrey, John, *Brief Lives* (ed. Dick, O. L., London, 1950), p. 200.

[3] Biondi wrote to Carleton about him: 'Every saint must have his candle but he offers none save to the godhead alone', that is, he devoted himself too much to James, and not enough to those near him.

[4] Wotton was more than a letter-writer. Cowley said of him:

> For, in whatever land he chanc'd to come
> He read the men and manners; bringing home
> Their wisdom, learning, and their piety.

All his days he had to take orders from others. In the last stanza the poem goes on:

> This man is free from servile bands
> Of hope to rise or fear to fall.

He had done nothing else but hope to rise and he knew something about falling.

XI

The reader of Chamberlain gains little respect for the Court of James I. The vulgarity of the courtiers and of the great ladies was evident not only in their ostentation but in their manners and morals. The Lord Mayor gave a supper and play to the Knights of the Bath and some of the knights carried themselves insolently in divers ways

> but specially in putting citizens' wives to the squeak, so far forth that one of the sheriffs brake open a door upon Sir Edward Sackville, which gave such occasion of scandal that they went away without the banquet.[1]

What was happening behind doors Chamberlain leaves largely to Carleton's imagination. The young men of the Court were no worse than many of the great ladies. In the MSS. Department of the British Museum are two volumes of doggerel verse about

[1] The playwrights knew of such episodes. In Jasper Mayne's *The City Match* (Act IV, Scene 3) Timothy is made to say:

> If that be all,
> I'll court her as if some courtier had begot me
> I'th'gallery at a masque.

Carleton wrote to Winwood in January 1604 (Winwood, *Memorials*, II, 43) about a masque: 'There was no small loss that night of chains and jewels and many great ladies were made shorter by the skirts.' See also Peyton, Edward, *The Divine Catastrophe* (1652), p. 47. Peyton was not the most impartial of witnesses. See also Carleton to Chamberlain, January 7th, 1604. S.P. 14/12, No. 6.

the scandals of the reign of James I and few of the well-known female figures escape aspersion.

Chamberlain must have been ashamed of his generation as he watched the doings of the Howards. Thomas Howard, Earl of Suffolk, used his office as Lord Treasurer to rob the Government. His uncle, Henry Howard, Earl of Northampton, was Lord Privy Seal and one of the most despicable of men, and was almost certainly involved with his niece in the murder of Overbury.

It is, however, the story of that niece, Frances, that shows the Howards at their worst. As a young woman she had been married to the Earl of Essex, son of the Elizabethan Essex. Essex was sent abroad for two years and his girl-wife became interested in Robert Carr, the handsome Scot whom the King had taken up. When Essex returned from his travels Frances refused to act as his wife. Chamberlain was told that a divorce was to be sued for and that Essex was said to be content (whether feigned or not) to confess 'insufficiency'. Chamberlain a little later reported that the Countess had had conferences with a 'wise woman', and had paid her much money. When the woman was clapped into prison for stealing a jewel from the Countess she countered by accusing the Countess of having dealt with her to make away with her husband, Essex. In the light of later events Chamberlain's story sounds not improbable. 'Great folks', he remarked, 'to compass their ends have neither respect to friends nor followers.'

James was eager to grace the Howards and to please his favourite. What could be better than to have Carr allied with so powerful a family? An ecclesiastical commission was appointed including the Archbishop of Canterbury and the Bishop of London to investigate the whole matter and of course to facilitate the divorce. In the meantime Chamberlain wrote:

> The lady hath been visited and searched by some ancient ladies and midwives expert in those matters, who both by

inspection and otherwise, find her upon their oath a pure virgin, which some doctors think a strange asseveration.

The Commission was slow to act, even to please a King in a hurry. Pressure was put upon them and at length by a vote of 7 to 5, the Archbishop being one of the minority, the Commission gave the Countess her freedom. Frances Howard was wed in white as a virgin to the favourite, now created Earl of Somerset. The King and Queen graced the wedding and there was a great masque. Many presents were given by the Merchant Adventurers, the East India Company, the Farmers of the Customs, etc., who knew what was expected of them.

Within three years the Countess and her husband were accused of having poisoned Sir Thomas Overbury and were sent to the Tower to await trial. Overbury had done his best to dissuade Carr from marrying Frances Howard and had in consequence incurred her hatred. The Countess confessed her guilt but Somerset stoutly denied that he had any knowledge of or part in the murder. The King was terribly upset lest his former favourite give away some secret and arranged that Somerset's testimony should be cut off at any time. He probably promised Somerset that, if he behaved properly, he and his wife would not be executed. They were condemned to death but were let off with imprisonment, though several of those who had assisted the Countess were put to death. The couple spent a few years in the Tower and were eventually released but played no more part in public life.

The story is not an appropriate one for assignment in girls' schools. Yet I have left out most of the unsavoury details and Chamberlain only touched upon them. In all of them James was interested. So was the Court, so was all London. No play had more spice in it, no play had a more striking dénouement. Chamberlain was careful as to what he set down on paper and confined himself fairly closely to known facts. He did not gloat over them; rather he hurried over them, as if ashamed of the Court.

Chamberlain was almost as disgusted with the intrigues of the Court as with its morals. He commended Sir Dudley Digges that he should be close in the country and avoided the court fever of hope and fear which continually tormented those dependent upon the great and their promises. Even the promises of friends were to be taken with reserve; they might play a 'trick of trust'. Chamberlain had lived too long and seen too much to think anything strange. The sudden shifts of favour, a wind from a new quarter, who could detect sooner than he?

He had watched the struggle for the Secretaryship from 1612 to 1614:

> Here is such discoursing, such working, plotting, and supplanting that what stands right today is awry tomorrow, and every day brings new alterations, so that they are driven to hammer and square out new projects . . . they say it is a pleasure for a man not interested to look upon gamesters, but in good faith I am so wearied with these varieties of discourse that I think it a miserable distraction and torture both of body and mind.

The poet Edmund Spenser had thought much the same:

> What hell it is, in sueing long to bide,
> To lose good days, that might be better spent,
> To waste long nights in pensive discontent,
> To speed today, to be put back tomorrow.

Spenser said it better than Chamberlain. His experience had been a personal one.

XII

Chamberlain watched the conduct and carriage of all women connected with the Court with the eyes of an old bachelor. The progress of courtships was worth sentences or even paragraphs. In February 1616 he mentioned the Countess of Bedford (Lucy Harington by birth) who is remembered because she was the patron of John Donne, of Ben Jonson, of Samuel Daniel and of Michael Drayton, as well as one of the most acquisitive of 'projectors'. As a matchmaker she was almost a professional and was occupied at the moment in furthering the romance of Lucy, younger daughter of the Earl of Northumberland, and James, Lord Hay. We have the whole story from Chamberlain. Hay was far engaged in affection and found acceptance at the hands of the young woman and of her mother. He had been two years a widower, was a Scot who had lived much in France, and was experienced in the ways of courts, 'a very sufficient, bountiful, complete and complimental gentleman'.

The young woman he courted was a creature of good looks, of spirit, and of guile, who was destined to remain a figure in English life for more than a generation and to become the friend of both Wentworth and Pym. Her father, that Earl of Northumberland who had been a prisoner in the Tower for many years, was an astrologer and a chemist and a man odd enough to be amusing. Moreover he was a friend of Ralegh, another prisoner, and figured largely in the society that had grown up in the Tower. He had no mind to see his daughter married to an upstart Scot. He was a Percy, he declared, recalling the older Border wars between the Percys and the Scots, and he could not brook it that his daughter should dance any Scottish jig. To prevent the marriage he summoned his two daughters to the Tower, dismissed the eldest, Dorothy, Lady Sidney, and told

Lucy that he was resolved not to part with her, and that her sister was to see to it that Lucy's maid and her clothes were brought to the Tower. Chamberlain had been told that the Earl had promised his daughter £20,000 to follow his wishes and drop Lord Hay, no inconsiderable inducement.

But the Earl forgot that Frances Howard, Countess of Somerset, was also in the Tower. That lady arranged for meetings between Lucy Percy and Lord Hay. When her father found out what was happening he dismissed his daughter and called the Countess by an ugly name. Lucy's mother, who, up to this point, seems to have furthered the match, refused to antagonize her husband by receiving her daughter, who was forced to take shelter with her sister, Lady Sidney.

The lovers could not marry at once because the King, who had promised to give away the bride, was in Scotland. Chamberlain says that Hay was wonderfully attentive and obsequious to his inamorata and spent the best part of his days at her dwelling. Three months later Lucy Percy and Lord Hay, who was to become Viscount Doncaster and later Earl of Carlisle, were married in the King's presence and before long the new Lady Hay was appearing in a masque as the Queen of the Amazons, accompanied by her elder sister.

Other courtships Chamberlain watched eagerly. Tom Hatton was wooing the widow of Sir Robert Ashton.

> He daily mans her to church, to plays, through the streets to the Exchange, plays at cards with her till after midnight, rides with her into the country, lends her horses.

Chamberlain added that the widow would be twice a week in Tom's chamber before he was up, and he did not even raise his eyebrows at such conduct.

Marriages interested him as much as courtships. He was almost as faithful in reporting approaching unions and disunions as Walter Winchell. Sir Arthur Ingram, the picker-up of concealed lands and of concessions of every kind, was to marry, and Chamberlain remarked of the bride: 'She hath withstood an army of wooers and, I think, is now lighted on the worst.' He had been told of Lady Ellesmere's conversations. Lord Ellesmere the Lord Chancellor, was ill and his wife anticipated his death, and

> makes a question whether she should incline to marry again, but if she did, she would willingly do it, so [on condition] that she might have no more children.

The reader may be a bit surprised that Lady Ellesmere was so forward-looking. I doubt if Chamberlain was at all surprised.

Ambitious women interested him, and that meant a wide range of interests. Of one he remarked: 'There being no doubt that she looks for a day.' Of another, the daughter of his old friend, Lytton, he gave an obituary comment:

> She was grown a very proper woman, but loved this town too well, which in short time would have drawn her and her husband dry as well in purse as in reputation.

He was inclined to smile at the new Duchess of Lennox,[1] who 'takes state upon her (they say) after the old manner, which is out of date long ago'.

He was critical of women who failed to measure up to his conservative standards. Lucy Harington, the Countess of Bedford, who had pushed the marriage of Lucy Percy, had given up painting her face,

[1] The gossip was that after James became a widower the Duchess aspired to marry him. It was said that her first husband had left her much money and that then she had married the Earl of Hertford. She would talk to the Earl of her great ancestry and he would tease her: 'Ah, Frances, Frances, but how long is it since thou didst marry the vintner's son?' The Earl left her £5000 a year and she next became the wife of the Duke of Richmond and Lennox. In her will she provided that her gentlewomen and maids should wind up her body in those sheets 'wherein my Lord and I first slept that night when we were married'. *Arch. Cantiana*, XI, 225-50. Cf. Wilson, Arthur, *The History of . . . King James the First* (London, 1653), pp. 258-9.

> which, they say, makes her look somewhat strangely enough among so many visards, which together with their frizzled powdered hair, makes them all look alike, so that you can scant know one from another at first view.

He was kinder to other women. Of Lady Cope he remarked:

> I cannot but pity her now a little, that after the loss of her husband, must leave her daughter and her children . . . leave her fair houses and her port [high position], and betake herself to a poor cottage . . . wherein I commend her course and good mind that can so soon settle herself to it without grudging or repining.

The Lady Penistone, wife of Sir Thomas Penistone, who had caught the eye of the Earl of Dorset and given anxiety to his wife, was thought by Chamberlain to be 'a dainty, fine young lady', and Burghley's daughter he counted 'the finest gentlewoman about the Court, with £8,000 portion'. Would that we knew more about her that we might understand Chamberlain's standards of female excellence.

XIII

Chamberlain's religious attitudes were those of the average less devout Englishman of his time. He had lived forty-nine years of his life in the Tudor world and he accepted the state church and its doctrines and was not given to excessive zeal of any kind. He disliked extremes and was suspicious of over-indulgence in religious exercises, whether by Puritans or Romanists. When a sermon was suggested for the opening of the new session of the Commons in 1621 he remarked: 'It seems we grow into a superstitious opinion of sermons, as the papists do of the mass that nothing can be done without them.' He thought it an idle custom that when men from any given county had an annual feast together in London, the proceedings should be opened by a sermon.

It is not surprising that he had no leaning towards the 'precise faction'; his phrase, 'a nest of Brownists', gives a clue to his attitude towards the more extreme Puritans. Yet he resented the fact that in a masque at Court a Puritan was brought in to be flouted and abused.

He was not fanatic about the Catholics. Towards converts to their faith, like Toby Matthews, an old friend, he took a patronizing tone as towards the foolish and deluded. It had been his attitude towards the Carleton sisters when they were looking Romeward. 'That devilish conspiracy', the Gunpowder Plot, made him angry rather than fearful. When a house in Blackfriars, in which Catholics had been attending a clandestine mass, collapsed, he was shocked at the manners of the public.

> A number were hurt, maimed, and lost their limbs, which found little help or comfort at first, our people being grown so savage and barbarous that they refused to assist them with drink, aqua vitae, or any other cordials in their necessity, but rather insulted upon them with taunts and gibes . . . They were ready to pull and tear them out of the coaches as they passed to their lodgings or to the surgeons.

The proposed match with Spain and the later match with France gave him occasion to worry, as it did most Englishmen. 'Men's hearts', he wrote, 'begin to sink and fear that religion is in hard case as well at home as abroad.' In 1621 Gondomar, the Spanish ambassador, had arrived in London and was 'high on his tiptoes', insolent and arrogant even to Councillors of State and obviously in great favour with the Court. It was murmured that he had been granted a licence to transport three hundred pieces of iron ordnance and had actually transported three times as much. That story distressed Englishmen who believed that their ordnance was superior and gave them an advantage over their enemies, of whom the chief in their eyes was Spain.

All things seemed to Chamberlain to work together for Spanish success. In October 1622 came word of the loss of Heidelberg to the Spanish troops. Meanwhile, five Commissioners were said to be arriving to treat of the marriage of Prince Charles to the Spanish Infanta. Gondomar had gone home but was returning again to England, 'because, it seems, no man knows so well the length of our foot'. Then suddenly news was whispered from mouth to mouth, and Chamberlain wrote it quickly (February 22nd, 1623), that Prince Charles and the Duke of Buckingham had set off secretly for Spain. Everyone agreed, wrote Chamberlain, that the trip would be a costly and hazardous experiment. At Court it was made to appear that the venture was going to succeed. Every little while news would come that the Prince was about to be married. Ships were sent out to bring the new couple home and rooms prepared for them in London.

Of the success of the wooing Chamberlain continued to be sceptical. To him it seemed that the Prince and the Duke had put themselves under a great handicap and that the Spaniards would take advantage of them. Reports continued nevertheless to indicate that all was going well. Messengers had been sent to Rome to secure a dispensation from the Pope. The London public was worried lest the marriage would be followed by toleration of the Catholics.

Then in October of 1623 came the unexpected news. The Prince and the Duke had come home without the Infanta, had called the Council together and had refused to receive the Spanish ambassador. Soon it became apparent that the match was off and that the Prince and the Duke were breathing out fire against Spain.

Chamberlain described the demonstrations of joy in London, the tables set up in the streets, the hogsheads of wine and the bonfires. So pleased were people with the outcome that they forgot, or at least seemed to forget, that an English Prince and the King's favourite had been made ridiculous figures. It was a matter for laughter but the joke was on the English, who seldom found such jokes funny.

It was not long before rumours were going round that Charles was to be matched with a French Princess, who would also of course be Roman Catholic. Presently it began to be whispered that in the secret articles for the marriage with the French Princess toleration was to be granted to all Catholics. Chamberlain was no doubt aware that such toleration meant that Prince Charles had broken his promise to Parliament. In April of 1624 Chamberlain had written that the Prince had assured Parliament that if he married any woman of a contrary religion, 'there should be no manner of connivance [i.e. toleration] but for herself and her servants strangers'. In 1625 Chamberlain reported of the members of Parliament:

> They begin to mutter about matters of religion, that the King [Charles] promised them when he was Prince, that he would never contract any marriage with conditions derogatory to that we profess.

Chamberlain added:

> They desire to understand what hath passed in that point, and the keeping them close makes them suspect the more.

Some of the leaders of the House of Commons had found out about the secret agreement with France and had set it down in their minds that they would never trust Charles.

The dissatisfaction in Parliament seemed to Chamberlain reasonable:

> Some spare not to say that all goes backward since this connivance in religion came in, both in our wealth, valour, honour, and reputation, and that it is visibly seen that God blesses nothing we take in hand, whereas in Queen Elizabeth's time, who stood firm in God's cause, all things did flourish.

Like many others he looked back wistfully to a happier time. A sermon of John Donne had been well received because it did Elizabeth great right, and another by an Oxford scholar won approval because the preacher was not long in commendation of the time but gave Elizabeth her due. To Chamberlain November 17th, the day of Elizabeth's succession to the throne, was to be looked upon as the happiest day England ever had. He was beginning to fear that evil days were ahead.

XIV

The political issues, like the religious, were only slowly being defined. The two alliances, that between King and Church and that between Puritans and Parliament, had not been fully cemented. Yet from the beginning of the reign of James the House of Commons, made up largely of men of puritan leanings, had been pushing for a larger share in policy. With the claims of the Commons Chamberlain had a certain sympathy, if they were not pressed too far. He was really afraid that the royal prerogative might be stretched too much. When the question of impositions on trade, that is, of new Customs duties without consent of Parliament, was to the fore in 1610 he thought the royal power strained so high that the English were likely to lose that freedom they had received from their forefathers.

Yet Chamberlain was a moderate to the core. He could not

approve the intransigence of successive parliaments, and thought the Sovereign had shown patience in dealing with the session of 1614. The right of parliament to grant money he recognized as a fundamental and long-established one, but hoped nevertheless that the Commons would see their way to supplying the real wants of the King. It worried him that Parliament continued 'stiff'. Slowly he came to lose faith, as Sir Thomas Wentworth later, in its capacity to make policy. The members had too many hares on foot at once. Early in the reign of James I, Chamberlain had made one of the most acute observations about Parliament (one often quoted) that the King had lost ground because he did not have more Privy Councillors in the Lower House. In 1624 he made another interesting comment, that the constituents were listening less to letters from the great and were making their own choice of representatives.[1]

XV

The economic situation of the country Chamberlain understood perhaps better than its political. He could see that James was running the Government into near-bankruptcy. The resources of the King, such as Crown lands, were being thrown away on favourites and their relatives and friends. Patents and monopolies that handicapped merchants and raised the price of

[1] In the early seventeenth century, as today, new members had to learn how to address the House of Commons. In 1614 Sir Ralph Winwood, as the new Secretary of State, suddenly found it his duty to lead the Commons. He had never been a member of that body and did not have the 'feel' of it. His first speech, although to the purpose, was in Chamberlain's view somewhat academical in tone. His second speech was regarded as better than the first. The House of Commons, Chamberlain observed, was a great school-house where his friend would meet many cross-blows. In criticizing a member of the Commons for being too academical and in suggesting that it was hard to hit exactly the right note in the House of Commons, Chamberlain was talking like a nineteenth-eentury newspaper man at Westminster. I can think of no one else in the early seventeenth century who recognized the problem before a speaker in the House of Commons.

living for everyone were being distributed to those who could gain the ear of the Sovereign. Chamberlain wrote:

> Many new patents come forth and more daily expected, as first for tobacco, whereby the new plantations of Virginia and the Bermudas are like to be stifled as it were in the cradle, another for saltpetre ... is not like to be lighter or less burdensome in the Lord of Buckingham's hands, another for scouring and trimming of armour throughout England, another for sixpence a load of hay of all that comes to this town by land or by water, another for whatsoever printed but on one side, whether in paper or parchment ... another for printing of linen ... another in hand for the probate of wills, which raises a great clamour among the proctors against Kit Villiers, who is to have the benefit.

This was in 1620, but Chamberlain was naming only a few of the many patents that had been granted.[1]

So many patents had been made to the Countess of Buckingham, the mother of the favourite, to this and that member of the Villiers 'kinred', that the Court had become a happy hunting ground for male and female adventurers, who could hope to become rich quickly. Buckingham learned that the East India Company was doing well and demanded £10,000 from them as a special gift. The merchant class and the public in general were the victims of the Court.

Some of the new schemes were worse than a tax upon the public. One of them proved a body blow to the country. The Merchant Adventurers shipped unfinished cloth to the Low Countries where it was given the final processes. Sir William Cockayne developed a project to make the finished cloth in England, and thus take away from the Dutch, who were the great

[1] See a sly allusion to Buckingham and the patents in *Westward Ho!* Birdlime says: 'Thankes, sir, I know you well, for all the kinred of the Monopolies are held to be great fleecers.' Again and again Chamberlain refers to the 'kinred' of Buckingham.

continental salesmen of woollen cloth, their finishing task. Chamberlain knew enough to realize that the plan was fallacious:

> The Merchant Adventurers have two days since voluntarily delivered up their charter to the King, and the new company have all at their will, yet they are already puzzled, for that the clothiers begin to complain and make petitions for want of utterance of their cloth, which beside all other in commodities abroad, may turn to a matter of dangerous consequence at home . . . It is found strange that the wisdom of the state could be induced to remove such a corner-stone upon so weak assurance as the vain promises and projects of idle brains.

Chamberlain hit the nail on the head. A little later he wrote that the major part of the Privy Council were opposed to Cockayne and his company but the King carried the day. Then he tells how the King dined at Alderman Cockayne's, where he was presented with a bason of gold and as many pieces in it as together made up a sum of £1000, the Prince after the same manner with £500.

Eventually the Cockayne project had to be given up and the Government had to renew its grant to the Merchant Adventurers. Meanwhile, however, England lost much of its woollen trade with the Continent and never wholly recovered from the interference with an established form of business.

The conditions that followed were observed by Chamberlain: 'It is most certain that England was never so generally poor since I was born as it is at this present.' No one was buying and many dealers were going bankrupt. Thousands of workers in wool were idle.

XVI

Chamberlain was mildly interested in English dependencies and in foreign countries and foreigners, perhaps more so than the average Englishman.

The chronic troubles with Ireland distressed him. 'The messengers come daily (like Job's servants)', he wrote in 1593, 'laden with ill tidings of new troubles and revolts', and a quarter of a century later he was considering how easily a foreign force might gain a foothold in Ireland. He regretted that the English had not done more to bring the Irish people to civility and religion, that is, of course, to the Protestant religion. The 'wild Irish' the English called them.

Chamberlain was dissatisfied with the English management of Virginia. In 1612 he entertained fears that the plantation at Jamestown would fail, through the 'extreme beastly idleness of our nation', a point of view about his own country that he perhaps picked up abroad. He shared the general disappointment when ships returned from Virginia without rich cargoes. When 350 colonists were reported massacred in 1622 through their own supine negligence he remarked that they lived as carelessly and securely there as if they had been in England. His annoyance was not entirely disinterested, for he was a stockholder in the Virginia Company, but its failures touched his pride of Englishry as well as his pocketbook. 'The disgrace and shame', he wrote, 'is as much as the loss, for no other nation would have been so grossly overtaken.' In that comparison he was doubtless overstating the case, but talking like the modern Englishman, who with all his deep-seated nationalism can be very critical of his own country.

His pride was hurt by the Dutch massacre of the English at Amboyna:

> I know not how we that have been esteemed in that kind more than other nations, do begin to grow by degrees less than the least, when the basest of people in matter of courage dare brave and trample upon us. I have known the time when they durst not have offered the least of those indignities we have lately swallowed and endured.

Yet he was not quite always critical of the foreign nation. In 1600 he regretted the quarrel with Venice: 'I am sorry we should have any difference with a commonwealth so generally esteemed for justice and wisdom.'

His curiosity about foreigners was not as much as might be expected of one who had been at least twice abroad and who corresponded with a diplomat. His attitude towards them was slightly patronizing, like that of the untravelled Englishman of our day. Londoners were accustomed to the sight of strangers but regarded them as a kind of sideshow. The Muscovy ambassador had taken his leave like a dancing bear. The ambassador from the Duke of Savoy had made no great dainty of himself but had gone with his entourage to the ordinary plays and to the Exchange and had chaffered and bargained in every shop. The Venetian ambassador had masked the declining importance of his state by a spectacular display of pomp. The Dutch Commissioners were flouted by the people who said that brawn was likely to be cheap this Christmas since so many boors were come to town.

XVII

Chamberlain liked to leave London, 'this misty and unsavoury town', but not for long. It is pleasant to know that in his last years he received recognition for his interest in his city. He was made a member of the Commission to undertake the repair of St.

Paul's. It was an unwieldy body of sixty-six members; privy councillors, bishops, aldermen, 'and for want of better, Master Wymark and myself that am very unfit for any such employment, and I know not how I came in unless it be for my love of the place'. The King, he added, is 'very earnest to set it forward, and they begin hotly enough', but he suspected, with Chamberlain cynicism, that it would prove 'as they say, Paul's work'. St. Paul's was in a bad state and so was London generally, in his judgment. He took little pleasure in walking abroad, 'to see the decay and desolation of this town, without hope in my time to see it better'.

To read Chamberlain is to understand how much *kleinestädterei* there was about the City he looked upon. London was not large and little episodes delighted the citizens. A man tied in a sack hopped from Charing Cross to St. Paul's; another managed to get himself and his horse on top of Paul's steeple;[1] two footmen engaged in a marathon from St. Albans to Clerkenwell, with the Court and the King interested in the outcome. It was said that Buckingham had won £3000 on the match. In the fall of a house at a puppet play two handsome whores had been killed. A cuckoo had flown over the pulpit at Paul's Cross during the sermon and had lewdly called out. In 1621 the Thames was twice frozen over in one winter and the watermen who had expected to make money during the parliamentary session were left with few fares.

The theatre, then as now so much of the London scene, did not interest Chamberlain. There was enough of the dramatic for him in the Court of James I. In 1614 the new Globe had been opened and Chamberlain reported that it was the fairest theatre that ever was in England. If he lived seven more years he might make a journey to see it. If Chamberlain had made journeys to the

[1] Cf. Dekker, *Dramatic Works*, III, 347, *Northward Ho!* also I, 194, *The Untrussing of the Humorous Poet*.

theatre and recorded his impressions, literary historians would long since have spread his fame. He stayed at home but in 1615 he wrote that plays were being given at the Court every night and that the audiences were going away in discontent. It seemed to him that the brains and inventions of poets were going dry and that they were compelled to refurbish old plays in order to make a profit. No doubt he would have blamed Shakespeare for making over old plays. Ben Jonson he mentions now and again and seems to have understood that he was highly regarded.

Yet he was not aware, so far as his letters show, that literature was being written in his city. This man, who had a considerable knowledge of classical writers and who quoted Chaucer, had little interest in contemporary Londoners who were writing plays and verse. Dr. Donne was to be made Dean of St. Paul's and he quoted someone as having said that if Ben Jonson were made Dean of Westminster, that church, Paul's and Christ Church (where Richard Corbet was Dean) should be furnished with three very pleasant, poetical deans. But writing poetry did not seem to him quite the thing for a man of position. He sent Carleton some of Donne's lines upon the death of the Marquis of Hamilton and admitted that they were reasonably witty (intelligent) and well done 'yet I could wish a man of his years and place would give over versifying'.[1]

He marked changes in the streets of London. Booksellers, stocking-makers and point-makers (who made a tagged lace for attaching hose to the doublet) and other men's trades were creeping into Goldsmiths Row, that was wont to be the beauty and glory of Cheapside. In other words, a district given over to the bankers of the time was being invaded by small retailers.

The less pleasant aspects of London life obtruded themselves

[1] On February 20th, 1609, Carleton wrote Chamberlain (S.P. 12/43, No. 81): 'I do much marvel at John Donne's ambition, but I do not well understand whether he seek for the Secretaryship of the grave Council of Virginia in London or that he means to be a traveller into the country.'

on the letter-writer. The apprentices celebrating Shrove Tuesday, the end of Lent, sometimes passed the bounds of frolic and fell to rioting. They were like to be hanged, Chamberlain reported, and deserved the penalty. He felt sorrier for the men caught by the press-gangs who were out recruiting soldiers for Mansfield's expedition in defence of the Dutch and of the Palatinate. The poor rascals, who knew from their fellows that starvation, disease and death probably awaited them, were being driven rather than led to Dover. One man hanged himself, one ran into the Thames and, after much parleying with the constables when he found that he could not escape the clutches of the press-gang, drowned himself; another cut off all the fingers of one hand, and still another put out his eyes with salt.

Again and again Chamberlain noted the incidence of the plague and sometimes gave figures as to the number of deaths per week. He made one interesting comment. The sickness killed few of 'the better sort'.

XVIII

In earlier pages I have given some space to the recipient of most of Chamberlain's letters, but there is something to add about the later Sir Dudley Carleton. All his letters to Chamberlain and many of his other letters I have skimmed through, skipping only the passages concerning continental politics and diplomacy. As the letters carry on into the early 1620s, they become a shade more formal and possibly somewhat less personal. Carleton was becoming progressively more absorbed in the European scene, as his job demanded, and as was to be expected of one who had lived abroad for years. About his friends and relatives in England he had less to say and Chamberlain seemed further away than once. To be sure, there were still expressions of affection for his old friend, but they were not as spontaneous. He was not giving as much thought to his old news-purveyor and he was not at pains to follow up cues Chamberlain had given him. To put him down as ungrateful would not be fair. He had many diplomatic epistles to send off and writing to Chamberlain was one more thing to do. Moreover a new group was running affairs in London, a group with which Chamberlain was not much in touch and thus unable to offer inside gossip.

Chamberlain was still on frank terms with his friend. On November 16th, 1622, Chamberlain had written:

> I remember I have heard more than once that your continual and earnest soliciting somebody's business hath done you more harm than good to the parties or cause you seek to advance, wherein I cannot but commend your noble and generous disposition that cannot forsake a good cause though it want success.

Carleton did not overlook his friend's frank words:

> You tell me of somewhat concerning myself; and I must yield unto you that I find small fruits of my indeavours; but a man must not take *manum ab aratro* [hand from the plough] for an ill-hazard, which it is in God's hand only to bless, when he seeth His time; which I, for my part, will attend with patience. Meanwhile I pray you believe that neither opiniatritie [obstinacy] or private design, or any particular humour doth lead me; but only that which I conceive to concur with my public duty; and, if I live long enough, I shall have my part of the reward of good deserts. If I die betimes (as I thought I should have gone the last week, of a fit of the stone) I will die with the reputation of an honest man.[1]

[1] In 1616 Chamberlain wrote Carleton: 'I see no man intends anything in public that doth not in some way concern himself.'

Well spoken, Sir Dudley! Few men in the great world of Jacobean politics ever had such sense of duty. Whether Sir Dudley was as high-minded as he thought himself, I cannot say for certain, but I find in his letters indications of a policy and of an ideal. At another time he wrote: 'I have the better contentment in all public business by how much I spare of my private benefits.'

Carleton did wish to get on, of course, but he did not cringe to superiors in order to do it. He was not given to assuring them that the only interest of his life was loyal service to their good. To the royal favourites, to Robert Carr and later to George Villiers, he had to send reports, but he addressed them less often than his immediate superiors, and, when he did write to them, avoided largely the personal note and dealt succinctly with the diplomatic problems in hand. In that respect his letters form a contrast to most of the state letters of the time, where men who should have been proud, indulged in abject flattery.[1]

It has to be admitted that Carleton was not above accepting money for favours done. The East India Company was distributing largesse among courtiers for benefits conferred and Chamberlain wrote of some who had been gratified largely. Carleton believed that in his diplomatic negotiations with the Dutch he had been helpful to the East India Company. Chamberlain had not been shy in calling attention to the claims of his friend and was given to understand that something would be done. But the East India Company moved slowly and Carleton wrote to Chamberlain that he was not content that the Commissioners who had negotiated with the Dutch should be treated so generously and 'the prime instrument . . . wholly forgotten'. He went on: 'I am not insensible of such a neglect and sooner or later I may have opportunity to make it appear', words that come close to a

[1] John Williams, Lord Keeper, and a good deal of a man, wrote letters to Buckingham that are sickening in their servility. Northampton's letters to James I are full of sugary flattery.

threat. Eventually Chamberlain was able to write that he had two hundred gold jacobuses in hand for him. A jacobus at that time was worth about twenty-four shillings. In a time when many officials were receiving gifts it is not surprising that Carleton wished a share of money from a Company that was making a great deal. We may regret that he was not above accepting such remuneration but we should be asking him to be more scrupulous than most men of his time.

XIX

It has been observed that Chamberlain was interested in the rise and fall of men, in the anatomy of careers. He would fain know how things were going for this and that figure. Was Sir So-and-so on the upgrade or past it and now on the down slope? Had he timed matters aright for his best success, had the fates in their spinning given him the choicest wool? Like his contemporaries with their inheritance of classical and medieval lore he was seldom forgetful of the workings of Fate and Fortune.[1] Many men lived too long for their reputation and would have been lucky to have gone years earlier. Others deserved well but took the wrong turning. Still others would have fared better had they lived in another age.[2]

How was it that this connoisseur of careers wished nothing for himself? His own modesty and want of ambition appear again and again. Yet he knew the pull that power has on men and he alluded in a letter to Carleton to 'the pleasure of dealing in great

[1] People talked much about fate and the stars. Sir Rowland Lytton wrote a letter to Carleton in 1602 in which he discussed Carleton's future: 'I know not how methinks your course hath hitherto been drawn or driven by a strange star, which hath not so crossed you that it may be counted malignant, nor yet hath given success to your projects.' In a letter to Chamberlain Carleton referred to the planet that reigned 'over our small house', and regarded it as an unhappy one. S.P. 78/46, f. 129v.

[2] 'Seeing preferment comes . . . rather to those whose parts sort and agree best with the humour of the time.' II, 595.

and high matters', a phrase that Carleton picked up and mentioned in his return epistle. As one reads the context of Chamberlain's letter one perceives that, as usual, he was thinking only of Carleton's career.

Yet Chamberlain laid so much stress on his want of ambition that one suspects that he must at some time have deliberately renounced the pursuit of success. In 1614 he was writing to Carleton about the struggle for the Secretaryship which he had followed so eagerly because he was interested in Winwood's candidacy. But Sir Thomas Edmondes, with whom he had long been on good terms,[1] had come over from Paris, hoping to gain a Secretaryship. He understood that Edmondes had reported without leave and unlooked for,

> which is thought an office better becoming a courier than an ambassador, which may be greatly to his prejudice.

Then Chamberlain goes on:

> I should be sorry it were so, yet I hope he hath such reasons and friends that he may wade through it well enough,

by which he means, I think, that he anticipated Edmondes's failure to get the post and hoped that he had such apparent excuses for his arrival and such friends to explain it that he would not lose face or seem disappointed. Then he adds with true Chamberlain philosophy: 'For things are as they are taken.'

It is possible that Chamberlain's philosophy about saving and losing face, a point of view not uncommon in his time, explains in some degree his own avoidance of a career. It may well be that Sir Dudley in our imaginary conversation with him had the saddle on the right horse, to use the idiom of the time. So long as Chamberlain stuck to his role of observer his dignity was

[1] He was fond of Edmondes but sometimes amused at him. 'He is still the old true-hearted man, and steel (as he says himself) to the back', that is, utterly trustworthy.

maintained, he had undergone no setback, no public disgrace, to which men might point.

In other ways, too, he piques our curiosity. What sort of man was he, who tells us discreetly of the unseemliness of the men and women of the Court, who seems to take the world as he finds it, wasting no energy on moral indignation, and yet whose standards were much higher than those of the busybodies he describes?

We cannot easily penetrate his reserve. He made few allusions to himself and, when he did, told us little. His inner life was his own guarded secret. Yet it must have been interesting, for there was some philosophy in him, at least about the course of events and of men's lives.

In vain have I gone back and forth through his letters attempting to follow up the stream of words to the springs of thought. It cannot be done. It is to be said of him that he wears well. We can still admire John Chamberlain through thirteen hundred closely packed pages because he was a man of character.[1]

I have examined his figures of speech, as men do those of Shakespeare, to discover if his similes and metaphors might betray something of the man. His figures of speech are seldom individual; rather they seem to be those characteristic of Londoners in his day. But they are not city sayings: they are those of hunting and falconry and horseback riding, and of farming and seamanship. To hear Chamberlain talk one would pick him for a country person. 'To send trees to the wood', was a phrase that might have been used by any rural writer. 'To lead you away with the lapwing from finding his nest' suggests one who had watched the ways of birds, but was a common metaphor, used for example by the playwright, John Ford.[2] 'To see if anything

[1] One of my acquaintances, a great historian who knows Chamberlain's letters well, has no good word to say for him, at least in conversation. Chamberlain is perhaps too conservative for his taste. But even in conservative and conventional men there may be much to admire.

[2] *The Witch of Edmonton*, Act II, Scene 2.

would have risen worth the flying at', is of course an idiom drawn from falconry. Of a fair young woman he remarks that 'her suitor grows weary of hunting in a foiled scent that hath been haunted by so many suitors'.

He talks like a farmer. Again and again he says 'that someone is in the briars', meaning that he is in difficulty, or more nearly that he is 'in wrong'. At one time he suggests that the man in the briars will hardly get off without scratching. He uses other idioms of the field: 'While this grass grows the horse starves.' He goes into the farmhouse: 'He is left in the suds', 'Let them brew as they bake'.

Figures of the sea come naturally to his tongue: 'I can yet discern no turning of the tide but that the water runs still the same way', 'They must either pull down their sails, or sink, if foul weather comes'. Another time he writes: 'I will do as I shall find fit occasion, and sound the haven before I make offer to enter.'

Nearly all these figures of speech[1] and others that he uses are to be found in the plays and prose of the time. I doubt if one of them was his own. He talked the speech of Londoners, and Londoners talked the speech of the country, which was close at hand.[2]

Yet there is one figure of speech of which Chamberlain was fond that may indicate something about himself. He said that he could not see further into a millstone than others. That is precisely what he was always hoping to do, to see into a millstone, to learn what was not evident at a casual glance, to penetrate to the meaning.

That meaning for him was not to be found in an economic interpretation, nor in some common trend in a series of events.

[1] It is an interesting fact that in his later years Chamberlain did not use so many similes and metaphors as in his earlier.

[2] Chamberlain occasionally uses words and phrases that remind us of Shakespeare: 'Master Winwood was married . . . with much thunder, lightning and rain.' He tells us that Mistress Dove 'made a good end' (I, 236). Both idioms were probably in common use.

His was nearly always an explanation that involved persons. Some powerful figure or family was moving the pawns. Who and why, he asked himself, and it was not hard in the reign of James I to supply the answers.

But he did not proclaim the answer on the house-tops. In some half-sentence he hinted at an explanation. He wrote, for example:

> There be a number of fine young gallants about the Court, more than I formerly mentioned, specially young Bell and Ruckwood. This mustering of minions and pressing so fast forward, makes the world suspect that it is toward a turning water.

What Chamberlain meant was that some attractive young men were being pushed upon the attention of the King, so that the reigning favourite might be displaced. He was the typical Englishman of whom Kipling speaks:

> In telegraphic sentences, half nodded to their friends,
> They hint a matter's inwardness—and there the matter ends.

Not that Chamberlain's sentences were telegraphic. He set forth well-constructed full sentences, with clauses and dependent clauses. It was in the dependent clauses that he hinted a matter's inwardness.

Occasionally he hinted at matters by saying almost the opposite of what he thought. He was telling of the Countess of Buckingham, mother of the Duke, and mentions the gossip that the new Lord Chief Justice should marry into the 'kinred' of the Villiers family and then goes on:

> In truth she is to be commended for having such care to prefer her poor kindred and friends, and a special work of charity it is to provide for young maids, whereof there be six or seven more (they say) come lately to town for the same purpose.

Now great men and women were not uncommonly in that time praised for looking out for their kin, and Chamberlain was merely saying what many would have said, but Carleton would have detected the irony in his words. It was a method of speaking that Chamberlain had come to use in his later years as he had become more sophisticated.

Take him all in all Chamberlain was more like an Englishman of our times than any other seventeenth-century man of whom I can think. Many of his traits are those we associate with some of the English of today. His quiet, pervasive humour, rarely to be met with in his time, his unaffected modesty, his reserve about himself, his shyness in a crowd, his preference for a small group of friends, his pains to be utterly truthful, his acceptance of a situation, however bad, his stout confidence, which he would fain conceal, in the moral superiority of his countrymen, all these characteristics are to be found among the English of our century and of the last. No doubt there were in his time many others like him, but the letters they may have written have largely disappeared.

XX

The years were bringing losses to Chamberlain. It was one of the discommodities of age, he discovered, to lose one's friends. He had other reminders of the lateness of the day. He forgot to give Carleton an item of news. Although his information was still fresh and copious he had less zest for acquiring and relaying it. He heard that the States (the Dutch) were taking their leave and had made a kind of end, but the details he did not know, nor was he particularly inquisitive.

> Whether it be that continual bad tidings hath taken away my taste, or that infirmity of age grows fast upon me, and

makes me not to regard how the world goes, seeing I am like to have so little part in it, for about the middle of the month I began to be *septuagenarius*.

The evening was shutting in. He was growing idle and unwilling to take more pains than needs. Old friends he did not seek out at once, when they turned up. Lady Carleton was in town and he had not seen her, because he was too lazy to make a trip across London, nor had he sought out a certain messenger of Carleton's, since he was too old to seek out new acquaintance. He who had been the mainstay of many a country-house confinement fled from Ware Park when a grandchild was expected, because he did not care for gossiping and much company. When he ceased to be interested in gossip he was indeed showing his age. The grasshopper had become a burden.

His brother, Richard, had died and had left him as chief heir and executor.

Now am I left alone of all my father's children, *omnes composui*, the last of eight brothers and sisters, and left to a troubled estate, not knowing how to wrestle with suits and law business and such tempestous courses after so much tranquillity as I have hitherto lived in, and, which is worst of all, in a weak bottom, as no other was to be expected from a man that for twelve or fourteen years never looked to his reckonings, and therefore according to the proverb they have looked to themselves, and left little or nothing: but I must pass it over as I may and bid all good days adieu in this world, when I have most need of rest and quiet.

Even his old occupation was failing him. Young Dudley Carleton wrote to his uncle, Sir Dudley:

Mr. Chamberlain doth not joy in the world since his brother died, as he did before, and saith that in one month he is

> grown seven years older than he was. He is . . . disheartened from writing to your Lordship, not having, as he said, received more than one letter from you since Michaelmas, and having withal more business now than he was wont, and by consequence less leisure, he maketh a doubt whether he shall not give over writing altogether.

One cannot blame Carleton. He had many letters to write to the Court. But his letters to Chamberlain by their excuses for not writing and by their rather forced expressions of friendship betray the realization on his part that he was neglecting his long-time friend in favour of people more essential to his future success.

Fortunately, however, Chamberlain went on writing – habit was strong. Fortunately, too, he enjoyed better health than most of his friends of his own age. We know that he suffered from stone in the bladder, like Carleton, but to that ailment he makes no allusion, so far as I can remember, save to say that he had been feeling unwell.[1] We may guess that he tried few remedies. He had always distrusted the drastic course of purging recommended by the physicians of the time. Physic he had believed did more harm than good. He had resolved to trust himself to good order and government and let physic alone. The epidemics of the time, the plague and smallpox, he had escaped. But he began to find the cold a great enemy.

In 1626 Carleton returned from The Hague and Chamberlain's letters to him ceased, or at least have not been preserved. Two years longer he lived. His will was dated June 18th, 1627, some nine months before his death, and, unlike many such documents, was a suitable epilogue to his life. His gifts to charity, to the poor prisoners in Ludgate, in the Poultry and in Wood Street, and to the poor distracted creatures of Bedlam, his generous gifts to

[1] In 1623 he received official permission to visit 'the Spa' in what is now Belgium.

Carleton, Lady Winwood and Lady Fanshawe, to his own nephews and nieces and to other relatives and friends, provided no doubt as genuine pleasure to the giver as to the recipients.

It was no hardship for Chamberlain to part with worldly goods, he who had never asked for more than a comfortable sufficiency. As he had been uninterested in worldly honours while he lived, so he preferred that his funeral should be performed 'with as little trouble and charge as may be answerable to the still and quiet course I have always thought to follow in my life-time'. Even the customary plan for reconciliation with his Maker, coming from Chamberlain, takes on more than formal significance. It was not difficult for one to reconcile himself to death who had been so reconciled to the vagaries of life.

ANNE CLIFFORD

ANNE CLIFFORD

ANNE CLIFFORD was born two years after the defeat of the Spanish Armada (1588) and died only twelve years before the Glorious Revolution (1688-89). As a child she looked in on the Court of Queen Elizabeth and as an old lady she had correspondence with a Secretary of State of Charles II.

The Cliffords were part of English history and literature. Cliffords had killed and been killed in the Wars of the Roses and one had walked the stage in Shakespeare's *Henry VI*. Was it not a Clifford heir, who, to avoid Yorkist vengeance, was disguised and brought up as a shepherd and was the subject of a poem by Wordsworth? Was not Fair Rosamond, the friend of Henry II, a Clifford? Most of that lore and much else of Clifford traditions Lady Anne knew. The records of the family were in her possession and at night she would ask for them, like the Persian king, who, when he could not sleep, would call for the chronicles.

Lady Anne[1] was the daughter of George Clifford, Earl of Cumberland, and of his wife, Margaret Russell. Her father, handsome, and in his early years wealthy, would have attracted attention in any court and was not overlooked in that of Elizabeth. Like other courtiers he gambled and found it necessary to refill his purse. Privateering against Spanish plate fleets offered the possibility of quick returns as well as of royal favour. Twelve voyages he undertook or sent out between 1586 and 1598, 'for the service of Queen Elizabeth', as his daughter put it. It is to be said for him that he avoided none of the dangers and hardships of the meanest seaman. But his voyages were ill planned

[1] In this section I have made great use of George Williamson's careful biography, *Lady Anne Clifford* (Kendall, 1922) but not without using myself all the sources available in print. I shall follow Williamson in calling the great woman Lady Anne, the name by which she was generally known in her own Westmorland.

and ill carried through, and the upshot was that he lost a great deal of money and found himself heavily in debt.

Margaret Russell, the mother of Lady Anne, had been married by her father's arrangement to his ward, George Clifford, whom she had doubtless known in the various Russell homes. She had assented to the marriage rather 'on the ground of common good than any particular liking', at least so she believed after the event. The minds of herself and of her husband 'met but in contraries and thought of discontentment'. Her experiences before marriage had been unfortunate. Her mother had died in her infancy and she had been sent from one house to another. Her stepmother, whom she called her mother-in-law, had been less than kind; her two brothers had died. Her husband proved no support at all. She found herself suddenly in a strange, unfriendly world separated from all her friends,

> not one to comfort me . . . I with thought grew almost continually sick, looking as a ghost that wanted the soul of comfort.

The children that might have occupied her did not come and she feared would not. Her failure to furnish him with an heir may explain in part her husband's unfriendly attitude. Yet by and by she felt a child stir within her and in time had two fair sons. A daughter was born to her, the Lady Anne of this story, but shortly after, she lost both her sons. Eventually after some years her husband proved more husbandlike and would in letters address her as 'sweet dear Meg', as 'dear pledge' and as 'my only beloved wife'.

She was worthy of affection, a remarkable woman from a remarkable family. The Russells had won their position by brains and initiative and by usefulness to the public. They had known also what they wanted and had been unusually successful in getting it. Of her mother Lady Anne wrote:

> She was naturally of an high spirit, though she tempered it well by grace, having a very well-favoured face, with sweet and quick grey eyes, and of a comely personage. She was of a graceful behaviour which she increased the more by her being civil and courteous to all sorts of people . . . She had a great, sharp, natural wit . . . few books of worth translated into English but she read them . . . [She] was a lover of the study and practice of alchemy, by which she found out excellent medicines that did much good to many. She delighted in distilling of waters . . . for she had some knowledge in most kind of minerals, herbs, flowers, and plants . . . She would often say that the kindness of her friends towards her had been one of the most comfortable parts of her life . . . She had a kind of prophetic spirit in her in many things . . . [She] knew well that all in this world is but vanity.

We may make allowance for a daughter's admiration of her mother and yet recognize a woman of parts and character. After an unhappy girlhood and a no less unhappy early married life she may have seemed inclined to view this earth as a vale of tears, but she had many things to interest her and to save her from introspection. She possessed, moreover, a kind of understanding and insight which availed her much.

She needed them. Even in the middle years when her husband was showing at length some affection for her he was away much of the time on privateering expeditions. She missed him and she saw his ships come empty home. Her later married life proved no happier than the first years had been; even unhappier, for she was unable to hold her husband, and, what seemed worse, everyone knew it. He was essentially an undisciplined adventurer. Gallantry was in the air and faithfulness to a wife not greatly esteemed in the highest circles. Cumberland became the lover of a lady of quality. When he received the King and Court at Grafton he made it clear that his wife was no longer the mistress of his home. His estrangement from her continued until shortly before his death, indeed for a time he separated himself from her. His daughter wrote that when her father and mother did meet

> their countenance did show the dislike they had one of the other, yet he would speak to me in a slight fashion and give me his blessing.

Shortly before his death Cumberland wrote to his 'Sweet and dear Meg', 'out of the bitter and greedy desire of a repentant heart'.

His death was in 1605. The widowed Countess lived until 1616 reading constantly in the Book of Job. She had endured unhappiness and loss and now she received another blow. By his will the Earl left his daughter £15,000 but bestowed the greater part of his northern lands upon his brother, Francis Clifford, the heir of the earldom, with a reversion to his daughter if the male line should fail. The will went against old entails. King John had made a grant of large tracts of Westmorland to the Veteripont family, whose heirs the Cliffords became. That grant became a grant-in-entail by the reign of Edward I. The lands in Craven, in the West Riding of Yorkshire, were entailed by Edward II to the Cliffords. Furthermore the said grants were validated by Act of Parliament in the first year of Henry VII. Those grants provided that the lands were to pass from eldest child to eldest child throughout the generations, without reference to sex. No doubt the Earl had reasons of his own for willing the lands to his brother. He was heavily in debt to him and he may well have thought that his estate would be safer in the hands of one who was to wear the title belonging to the Cliffords. But he was going directly against a grant-in-entail, and his will was legally invalid.[1]

[1] The claims, however, on both sides, were complicated. The Cliffords had been attainted in the Wars of the Roses. Parliament had restored their rights. But a case could be made for the breaking of the entails.

Margaret Russell Clifford, now dowager Countess of Cumberland, believed her daughter deeply wronged; it became the object of her life to recover the northern lands for the rightful heir. She had all the records of the Veteriponts, the Vesceys and the Cliffords searched and believed that they confirmed without any doubt her daughter's claims. Lady Cumberland, wrote her daughter approvingly, never yielded to any opposition whatever.[1]

The daughter had to grow up in a none too cheerful environment. As she looks out at us from early portraits she appears a solemn little personage. In that face there seemed no possibility of childish glee and gaiety. The long struggle between her father and mother and the misery of the mother – there is nothing children catch so quickly – left their mark upon the impressionable girl. Something else is to be seen in that face. The eyes start from the head as if the child might have had thyroid troubles. From her youth on she was a restless creature; in her old age she was always moving from one castle to another, as if her inner spirit yearned for change. Yet even as a young woman she looked a poised person and one fully aware of her own position.

Her appearance as a girl she describes:

> I was very happy in my first constitution, both in mind and body, both for internal and external endownments, for never was there child more equally resembling both father and mother than myself. The colour of mine eyes were black, like my father and the form and aspect of them was quick and lively, like my mother's: the hair of my head was brown and very thick . . . with a peak of hair on my forehead, and a dimple in my chin, like my father; full cheeks and round

[1] That Lady Cumberland was not wholly stubborn but might have proved conciliatory was the opinion of John Bowyer in a letter to Francis, Earl of Cumberland. See Whitaker, T. D., *The History and Antiquities of the Deanery of Craven* (ed. Morant, London, 1878) pp. 367-8. It may be that Lady Cumberland hoped to make a good compromise settlement, but I suspect that Bowyer was too optimistic on that score.

> face like my mother, and an exquisite shape of body resembling my father.

She fails to tell us that she was very short. But we do learn that she was an ailing child and was sent to stay with old Mrs. Elmes, her great-aunt, at Lilliford House in Northamptonshire. There she believed that she was seasoned with the grounds of goodness and the love of a private country life. Her mother had brought her up in as much goodness and religion as her sex and years were capable of. But her mother was seldom in London and the daughter was often left in the care of her mother's much older sister, the Countess of Warwick, who was chief lady-in-waiting of the bedchamber, and for a long time, if we may trust Lady Anne, more beloved and in greater favour with the Queen than any other lady in the kingdom. No doubt that excellent Countess had much to do with training her niece in the ways and manners of the Court.

At an early age she was given a dancing teacher and an instructor in music. Her governess imparted to her not only knowledge but a love of knowledge. She had a further advantage. Samuel Daniel, scholar and poet, who wrote four of the masques performed at the Jacobean court, was retained as her tutor and instilled into the mind of the girl a love of poetry, and especially of the poems of Sidney and Spenser. Spenser's *Fairie Queene* she came to admire so much that she later paid for the monument to him in Westminster Abbey.

Her father had insisted that his daughter should be trained only in the English language and that she was not to study Latin. As she grew older her maids read to her from her favourite works. Sentences and passages that caught her fancy she had copied out by secretaries and pinned them on the walls and hangings and furniture of her rooms. They became part of her spiritual equipment and she tells us that she garnished her conversation with

ANNE, COUNTESS OF PEMBROKE, 1590-1676

them. It is a fair guess that many of those sentences were out of Roman writers and that she was influenced by Latin wisdom.

Her account-book from 1602 to 1604 when she was twelve to fourteen tells us something of her. Gifts were being showered upon her and she had to write letters acknowledging them and to reward the servants who brought them. She rewarded the one who found her lost looking-glass. Many purchases she made. For a wire frame for a ruff she paid 7s., for jersey stockings 4s. She bought two pairs of Spanish leather and some holland (linen) for dresses, flowers for her hair, a ring and a jewel, glass flowers and pendants of gold and pearl. An hour-glass cost her 4s. She purchased paper books for writing. She bought 'some little silk-worms', and she had already begun to make silk embroidery.[1]

When she was twelve years old there were good hopes, as she thought, that she would be appointed an attendant at Queen Elizabeth's Court. Those hopes came to nothing. The aged Queen fell ill, and little Anne would wait in the chamber outside while her aunt, Lady Warwick, watched over the Queen dying slowly at Richmond. Towards the end of March 1603 Lady Warwick advised her sister, Lady Cumberland, to move with her daughter into London in order to avoid the confusion that might occur on the death of a sovereign. It had been a long time since the death of a crowned head and no one knew what might happen. Thanks, however, to the smooth-working Robert Cecil every-

[1] 'In the second year of Queen Elizabeth, one thousand five hundred and sixty, her silkwoman, Mistress Mountague, presented her Majesty with a pair of black-knit silk stockings for a New Year's gift, the which after a few days wearing, pleased her Highness so well that she sent for Mistress Mountague and asked her where she had them, and if she could help her to any more, who answered saying I made them very carefully of purpose only for your Majesty, and seeing these please you so well, I will presently set more in hand. Do so, quoth the Queen, for indeed I like silk stockings so well because they are pleasant, fine, and delicate, that henceforth I will wear no more cloth stockings, and from that time unto her death the Queen never wore any more cloth hose.' Stow, John, *Annals*, 1631, p. 867b. The Continuation from 1603 to 1631 was by Edmund Howes. Where he got this story, which I have not seen elsewhere, I do not know. On p. 894a he tells about the development of the silk industry in Italy, and then in Spain and Portugal and then in France. He goes on to tell of the efforts by King James to introduce silkworms and mulberry trees into England. Howes says that in 1609 mulberry trees were planted in many shires.

thing went off peacefully and James VI of Scotland became James I of England (1603).

Much there was to interest a girl of thirteen. The Queen's body was brought from Richmond to Whitehall. Her mother and no doubt her Aunt Warwick were among the great ladies standing in the black-draped barge as it moved slowly down river one night. Lady Anne had hoped that she might be given the privilege of keeping watch by the coffin of the Queen but that opportunity she was wisely denied. The best she could do was to walk in Whitehall gardens exchanging gossip with other young people of rank. She hoped also to take part in the funeral ceremony but was again disappointed. She was not high enough. She did manage to gain a place in Westminster Abbey to see the service performed.

Her circle was of course intensely interested in the new King and in his Queen. Lady Anne's mother and her aunt, Lady Warwick, took the thirteen-year-old girl with them when they drove out to Theobalds to pay their respects to the King,

> who used my mother and aunt very graciously, but we all saw a great change between the fashion of the Court, as it now is, and of that in the Queen's time, for we were all lowsy by sitting in the chamber of Sir Thomas Erskine.

Lady Anne was obviously quoting her elders. Those elders were no doubt thinking also of a profounder change. They and their friends who had been close to the old Queen were now to be on the edge of the picture. The girl believed that her mother and her aunt were not in the good books of Sir Robert Cecil and of the Howard family.[1]

The court was a different place in other ways.

There was much talk of a masque which the Queen had at

[1] Cecil was of course at the King's right hand but it is surprising to think of the Howards as having as early as 1603 and 1604 the influence with the King which they later attained. Henry Howard was already a factor, and no doubt also Thomas Howard.

Winchester and how all the ladies about the Court had gotten such ill names that it was grown a scandalous place.

It was to continue to be such a place and the King was as much responsible as his Queen.

The teenage girl observed other things that concerned her more closely. There was a dispute between her father and Lord Burghley over precedence. It was settled in favour of the Earl of Cumberland and so, remarked the daughter, 'it lineally descended to me'.

The question of Lady Anne's marriage began to be discussed. She was, apart from her Westmorland lands, a considerable heiress. Rumours were going around that Robert Carr, already a favourite of James I, and later to be created Earl of Somerset, was to marry Lady Anne. When only fifteen Lady Anne had written her mother that her father had promised her that nothing should happen about any match for her without her mother's consent 'as a chief matter'. She realized that a young woman should defer wholly to her parents in the matter of marriage and she asked pardon for mentioning the subject. No doubt she hoped that her mother would see to it that she was not forced into a marriage against her will.

Five years after that letter Lady Anne was married to Richard Sackville, and privately in her mother's room, without banns. Three days after her marriage her father-in-law, the second Earl of Dorset, died, and the bride found herself Countess of Dorset and the mistress of Knole House, one of the great houses of England then and now.

About the courtship and marriage arrangements we know almost nothing. John Chamberlain wrote to a friend that Sackville had been in speech about Lady Anne in his grandfather's time, that is, at least as far back as 1608, a year earlier. He implies that Buckhurst, seeing his father about to die, hurried up the marriage in order to avoid falling into wardship. As for the young woman we can only guess that her mother approved of the marriage. After all Lady Anne was twenty years of age and it was quite time for her to be married. She was becoming a member of a comparatively new but already well-known family. Her husband's father had been Lord Treasurer and his grandfather an important Government official. The Sackvilles had gathered money and lands and were sometimes dubbed the Fillsacks.

Richard Sackville, the new Earl of Dorset, was a well-set-up young man, nearly a year older than his bride. At the outset he seems to have treated her with respect and kindness. Of him she always wrote in terms of praise, even when she was suffering from his commands, and ascribed to him a just nature, a sweet disposition and valour. He soon became a well-known courtier. He was expert in jousting, he had the gift of making himself liked, and he was said to be an intimate of the heir-apparent, Prince Henry. On all sides he was regarded as a coming man. But to be a coming man and a favourite of the King he had to offer sumptuous entertainment and to maintain a reputation as a bountiful person. At the wedding of the Princess Elizabeth to Frederick of Bohemia in 1613 display was in order and 'all speak of the Earl of Dorset'.

Dorset might, however, have gone on spending his substance without quarrelling with his wife. It was her claims to the northern lands that raised trouble between them. Lady Anne's mother led the fight for those lands; she began a suit in the Court of Wards in her daughter's name; later the case was taken to the Court of Common Pleas. At length the King offered to serve as an arbitrator. What that meant the dowager Countess of Cumberland understood only too well. James would decide in favour of her brother-in-law. It was a blow to mother and daughter to find that Dorset, eager to be on good terms with the Court, opposed his wife's claims and pleaded with her not to stand out against the King.

The King was doing his best to effect a final settlement of the lands. By a patent of the crown he granted to Francis, Earl of Cumberland, the uncle of Lady Anne, the reversion of the Clifford estates. In an action brought in the Common Pleas before four judges, Cumberland, his son Henry and Lady Anne's husband agreed to abide by the decision there to be rendered. To any such decision Lady Anne refused to be a party. Against entreaty and threats she stood firm. The Archbishop of Canterbury (George Abbot) walked with her for an hour and a half in the long gallery of Dorset House, trying his best to persuade her to accept the award of the judges. Many of her most intimate friends came to see her and pressed her to give way, 'sometimes terrifying me and sometimes flattering me'. She put them off, declaring that she would decide nothing until she consulted her mother in the North.

Northwards she turned, accompanied part of the way by her husband, who no doubt urged her to give up her claims on the lands. From Westmorland she sent word back that she refused to accept the award of the judges. At that point her husband forwarded commands that she should be left in the North. Lady Dorset was angered; she drew up a statement that her husband had ordered her to stay in the North, signed it herself and induced some of her friends among the neighbouring gentry to sign it with her.

When she returned to Knole she found but a 'cold welcome', from her lord and master. From then on she experienced much coolness from him mixed with occasional kindness at times when he still hoped to win her over. 'About this time', she wrote:

> I used to rise early in the morning and go to the standing [platform] in the garden, and, taking my prayer book with me, beseech God to be merciful to me in this and to help me, as he always hath done.

Things grew pretty black for her. Her husband played another card. He informed her that he was coming down to see her for the last time and that her child was to be taken from her to London and to be given in charge of the Comptons at Horsley in Surrey. Lady Compton was Dorset's sister and had been on good terms with his wife but was nevertheless on her brother's side in the controversy.

Dorset continued to mix threats and kindness. His wife heard that she was no longer to live at Knole or at Bolebroke but would have to reside at Little Dorset House in London. It was intimated to her that her child would not be brought any more to see her. Then Dorset would come down from London to Knole and be all graciousness, he would sit and talk with her about the people of the Court. He had been at a great gathering in Sussex with his brother-in-law, Lord Mordaunt, Tom Neville 'and all that crew'. Lady Anne was half pleased and wholly envious. What a gay existence her husband enjoyed:

> All and infinite great resort coming to him. He went much abroad to cocking, to bowling alleys, to plays and horse-races, and commended by all the world.[1]

She too, she knew, could enjoy London gaieties if she would only yield to her husband's wishes and gave up her northern claims. Meanwhile, she wrote,

> I stayed in the country, having many times a sorrowful and heavy heart . . . I am like an owl in the desert.

[1] Dorset was one of the greatest spenders of his time. Knole had a staff of something over a hundred. Lady Anne wrote of her husband's excessive prodigality in housekeeping. Aubrey, writing a good deal later, said that Sackville lived in the greatest splendour of any nobleman in England, and Clarendon presented him as a spendthrift. John Chamberlain wrote that when Dorset died he left debts of £60,000. His wife was always careful about money and did not enjoy seeing it thrown around. Moreover she observed that Dorset lost money constantly to the King at cockfighting and gambling and that he seemed to be gaining increasing favour with the King. She suspected that those two facts were not unconnected.

At this point the Countess of Dorset received word of her mother's death in the North. It was bitter news to her. She was left alone to fight her battle. Northward she turned to attend the funeral. On her return to Knole her husband seemed friendly. Presently he persuaded her to pass her lands in Westmorland to him, if she had no heirs. This was a slight concession but one that seemed to bring about better domestic relations.

But the Countess had more to go through. On January 18th, 1617, she had to appear before the King. The Queen, she knew, was on her side and had warned her not to trust any matters absolutely to the King lest he should deceive her. When she appeared before him James put everyone out of the room except her and her husband and appealed to them to leave the whole matter in his hands – James always fancied himself as an arbitrator. Dorset of course consented but Lady Anne replied that she would never part with her Westmorland lands while she lived. The King tried persuasion and then 'foul means', by which she probably meant threats, but 'nothing would move me'. On the twentieth of the same month the King made another attempt to beat her down, this time publicly. She found herself in a room with her husband, her uncle Francis, Earl of Cumberland, his son and various great figures of the Court, including the Earl of Montgomery (eight years later to become her husband), the Lord Chief Justice and two lawyers. The King asked the four principals if they would accept his judgment. Once more Lady Anne refused, 'at which the King grew in a great chaff'. It was a tense situation and her husband had the presence of mind to have her quickly escorted from the room lest she should receive some public disgrace from the Sovereign.

It is hard for us to realize the ordeal which Lady Anne had been put through. The King was all in all, his goodwill of infinite importance; he was asking her to leave matters to him, the wise old King of England, as he thought himself, and she had the effrontery to refuse. Her obstinacy must have seemed to the members of the Court incredible.

It is probable that the memory of the promise made to her mother that she would never yield her northern lands made it the easier for her to resist all the importunities of those around her and to stand out against the Crown itself. She had tenacity and courage beyond estimate.

Dorset came out from the meeting telling her that it was determined that, if she would not come to an agreement, there should be one without her. But he was so gracious to her that she went away in high spirits. Apparently she was relieved at the outcome, and we may imagine why. She had done her best, she had stood up to the mighty, she had kept her promise to the dead, and now the matter was in other hands.

The agreement finally worked out between Dorset and Cumberland involved payments at different times by Cumberland to Dorset of £20,000 in return for the renunciation of Lady Anne's claims. The £20,000 explains in part why Lady Anne's husband had pushed her so hard. As a courtier dependent upon royal favour he was eager to please the King but the prospect of ready cash at different times in the near future was hardly overlooked by one who was always spending more than his income. That Cumberland was willing to pay so large a sum tells us much as to the legal strength of Lady Anne's case and explains why so much effort was made to break down her resistance.

For a time the diary ceased to be that of a tortured young woman and dealt with her clothes, her books and presently with 'the child'. Since things had been settled against her she was allowed to have her child again.

Her first child had been born in July 1614, three and a half years before her ordeal with the King. It had been named Margaret in honour of her mother. Three other children Lady Anne bore but they all died in infancy. A fifth child, Isabella, was born in 1622. The diary is full of details about little Margaret. She fell ill with teething at Bolebroke in Sussex and a physician was summoned. The danger passed and the child began to 'prattle and go'. In the next year she had fits of ague and the mother could hardly sleep at night. In 1624, seven years later, the child had a serious case of the smallpox and the mother nursed her until she herself caught the infection.

The stages in the life of the child interested the mother. Clothes marked epochs: the first whalebone bodice, the first new red baize with lace on it. A day came when the leading-strings were taken off and the child could walk alone. On her fifth birthday her father ordered her health drunk throughout the house and her grandmother sent her some delicate little gloves and a rich jewel of diamonds.

During these years as Countess of Dorset there were two Lady Annes, the great lady taken up with company in London and the desolate wife filling in dull days at Knole.

The great lady was on a continuous round of calls. She dined with Lady Elizabeth Grey and her husband and the three of them went off to call on the Countess of Arundel and to view the paintings and sculpture which Arundel had brought from Italy. New Year's Day was a round of visits; Lady Anne called on the Queen and found friends there. She went on to visit the Countess of Northumberland, whose husband was a prisoner in the Tower, and to see Lady Rich. When George Villiers, the handsome new favourite, was created Earl of Buckingham, the Dorsets were present. They had supper with the Arundels and then went to see a new play, *The Mad Lover*.[1]

There were excursions to the Tower to see friends imprisoned there. More than once Lady Anne went to call on Frances Howard, Countess of Somerset, the cousin of her husband.

[1] By John Fletcher.

It was hardly curiosity to see a great lady in prison on a charge of murder that led Lady Anne to make such a visit; more probably she was unwilling to go back on a relative in adversity. Another friend whom she had known, the Countess of Suffolk, was also in the Tower for extorting money from those who had to deal with the Treasury, where her husband had been Lord High Treasurer. Lady Anne noted that the Countess of Suffolk had suffered from the smallpox which spoiled that good face of hers, which had brought to others much misery and to herself a greatness that ended with much unhappiness. Lady Anne was not above deriving satisfaction from the misfortunes of others, especially of the good-looking.

The days at Knole were less thrilling than those in London. Sometimes she was ill and stayed in her chamber. Once she forgot that it was a day of fasting and had flesh for dinner, for which she was properly sorry. To complete her ill luck she played at gleek and lost £27; she was often a loser at that game.

Her interest in everyday affairs saved her from boredom. There was the garden and the great park to walk in and cherries to pick. She mentions a sunrise, the arrival of new puppies, and the food for the cat. She plays barleybreak on the bowling green and spends much time on her Irish stitchwork. She makes elaborate embroidery which she could use as gifts. Now and then she joins the maids in the kitchen to stir up rosemary cakes, to mix pancakes and to make quince marmalade which she puts up and gives away as presents.

She was not without company and diversion. There were visits to pay in the neighbourhood and friends were constantly coming to see her. She went to inspect the flowers in Dr. Lune's garden. On a Sunday Sir Ralph Boswell dined at Knole and played and sang to her afterwards. The celebrated Dr. Donne, rector of Sevenoaks, whose sermons were being talked about, preached both morning and afternoon and she had his company at dinner.

We may infer from other evidence that she enjoyed talking with him and had much to say herself.

Like many Englishwomen out of country houses she did not always give her best mind to her clothes. Two months after her mother's death she was wearing a black silk grogram gown. Later she mentions a black taffeta night gown (a gown for evening wear) and a yellow taffeta waistcoat. When she reached London in December of 1616 she had a new black wrought taffeta gown made by Lady St. John's tailor. When she went down to Knole in the spring of 1617 she wore a white satin gown with a white waistcoat. Later on her London tailor carried out an order which she had left with him, and the Kentish villagers must have stared when they saw their lady of the manor in a 'sea-water green satin gown', or in a 'damask embroidered with gold', both with a green ruff of the French fashion.

Her husband moved through the pages of her diary. She observed his affection for his daughter and confessed that he deserved commendation in everything save in the business of her northern lands.

> Sometimes I had fair words from him and sometimes foul, but I took all patiently and did strive to give him as much content and assurance of my love as I could possibly.

His moods varied. He objected to her reading the Old Testament with Mr. Rand, the chaplain, because it interfered with his study. From all we know of the third Earl of Dorset, we cannot suppose that he gave up much time to study. Perhaps he went over accounts, for he complained to her that she had been left less money than he had been given to understand. He dined privately but supped with her. 'This night my lord should have lain with me but he and I fell out about matters', but the next night he came to her chamber. When he was ill in London she sent him letter after letter beseeching him to come to Knole that she might care or him. Too anxious to please him, too appreciative of his occasional and slight kindnesses, she allowed him the advantage. Her eagerness to prove a good wife is touching but made little impression on her husband. Always there was the sore point between them. He wrote her that in all things he loved her and held her a sober woman, 'your lands only excepted, which transports you beyond yourself and makes you devoid of all reason'. In other words he thought of her as unreasonable and excitable, faults often then attributed to women.

She had indeed a hard time and the sympathy of the reader goes out to her. To be threatened with losing her husband and never seeing her child again was unpleasant. The Earl seems to have been given to a refined and continuous cruelty to his mate, merely to gain royal favour and more ready money.

Yet it is conceivable that there was a little to be said for him. The Countess was not an easy woman to get along with. She quarrelled with her servants and with her equals, reproaching them sometimes passionately. She was either ill a good deal of the time or thought herself so. Once from mid-October 1619 to the end of March 1620 she shut herself in her room and would not cross the threshold. Perhaps she believed herself seriously sick or possibly she was subconsciously punishing her husband. At one time he asked her to take charge of the house and she refused, because things went so ill with her. What may have been even more irritating to her husband was her proneness to weeping. On Whit Sunday 1617 she went to church and her eyes 'were so blubbered with weeping' that she could scarcely look up. Such spells were not unusual with her. She was sorry for herself. She had not yet developed those resources within herself that she showed in later life. Sometimes tears are a potent weapon in bringing husbands round. In this case it was not so.

She was alone at Knole much of the time and was reduced to the company of servants. She could hardly forbear talking with them. She spent a day walking in the park with her laundry maid, Judith, carrying her Bible with her, and thinking and possibly talking of her troubles. She gave up walks and tried to set as merry a face as she could upon a discontented heart. In her craving for sympathy and support she persuaded herself that the men in the house loved her exceedingly. I am afraid that in reality some of those men relayed her complaints to her husband. In some ways she was an unpractised young woman, moving a little uncertainly among designing people, saved only by her singleness of purpose and sheer courage.

She seemed to find consolation in looking to the past; she liked to 'compare things past and present'. When matters were going badly for her she would read over the chronicles of the Clifford family or with an assistant work at the continuation of them. When a batch of books was brought from the North to be set up in her retiring room and she was troubled about the turn of events in Westmorland she talked of her dear mother and 'other businesses in the north'. She enjoyed conversing with men who knew her country and who could recall her father and mother; she liked to tell listeners about Queen Elizabeth. Moreover she took a sad pleasure in revisiting places connected with her own life and even in her younger years had a feeling for rooms which was to grow upon her in later life. In November 1617 she went to Austin Friars in London where she had lived with her mother at the time of Queen Elizabeth's death. 'I wept extremely to remember my dear and blessed mother. I was in the chamber where I was married.' A good cry seemed to steady her.

Her love of reading proved an ever present help. Exodus, Leviticus and Deuteronomy were read aloud to her. Many religious books were gone through including St. Augustine's *City of God*. The servants took turns in reading Montaigne to her. She found pleasure in Sandys's *Travels in the East* and in Grimstone's *General Historie of the Netherlands*. Leicester's

Commonwealth was full of gossip about the early Elizabethan period and she made notes on the margins of the pages. Her secretary tells us that she read most of the histories extant. The manuscripts of the Clifford family were always worth conning again, and she devised a scheme for drawing up a history of her father's life.

What her thoughts were about religion she does not indicate but she was at times devout and gave heed to spiritual matters. She indulged herself in one long conversation about religion. She attended church frequently, as became a lady with an example to set. Like others, she looked most to Providence when most worried. The Old Testament interested her far more than the New. She talked about her enemies in language that reminds one of the Old Testament. It distressed her to think that they were getting the upper hand of her. About the ways of Providence she once, in her later years, revealed in talking with Bishop Rainbowe a certain simplicity of outlook. He had told her that there was sure to be war with the Dutch, to which she answered:

> If their sins be greater than ours, they would have the worst.

That God supported in war those who served Him and rendered ineffectual the military efforts of those who offended Him she had learned from the books of Kings and Chronicles.

Only at one period in her life did Lady Anne exhibit the symptoms of religious distress common in her day. Those symptoms appeared at Knole in a time of enforced idleness and of bitter reflection. She had been reading devotional books and discussing them with her servants and began to grow more and more worried about her spiritual life. She took to fasting, and the young woman who had once forgotten a fast day prescribed for herself an even stricter diet than the church required. Butter and eggs she forswore during Lent, and her maid kept the fast with her. When her husband came down from London and objected to her regime she admitted that she looked pale and sickly and was easily persuaded to give up fasting.

But she was not quite done with the spiritual crisis. It was spring and Easter was approaching. After supper on Good Friday she fell into a great fit of weeping. The Earl was summoned and learned that his wife's spirit troubled her and that she was going to refrain from partaking of the communion this Easter. Her husband was inclined to take her scruples lightly as perhaps the display of a feminine mood. But when he learned that she had talked with her chaplain and was in earnest, he cancelled the service for himself and for the family. This was too much for Lady Anne who was going to miss the sweet sorrow of watching others partake when her conscience forbade her to do so. Next month she was in London and, for some reason, the religious fervour did not continue. There were other things to think about.

The death of Anne of Denmark, James's Queen, took the Countess of Dorset to London and offered agreeable excitement. She took her turn in watching over the Queen's body. On May 13th she was one of the mourners at the funeral and walked in the procession from Somerset House to Westminster Abbey. The funeral ended, as funerals often do, in cheerful meetings of friends. Lady Anne ran into old Lady Pembroke and others of her acquaintance with whom she had much talk. When all was over she went to her husband's sister, Lady Beauchamp, to show off her mourning attire.

Her husband became openly interested in another woman, Lady Penistone. For a time the Countess appears to have ignored the lady but in May 1619 her husband gave a supper for some friends of the French ambassador, followed by a play and a banquet, and among the guests was Lady Penistone. A few months later Dorset succeeded in compelling his wife to have a small party at Knole that included Sir Thomas Penistone and his wife.

> The 25th they stayed here all day, there being great entertainment and much stir about them.

During that same summer Lady Penistone went to Tunbridge Wells, not far from Knole, ostensibly to drink the waters, and Lady Anne set down in her diary:

> This coming hither of Lady Penistone's was much talked of abroad and my lord was condemned for it.

Within a few months Lady Penistone, a 'dainty fine young lady', as John Chamberlain calls her, was dead of the smallpox.

In March 1624 when Lady Anne was nursing her daughter, ill of the smallpox, she had word that her husband was ill in London. He assured her in a letter that nothing serious was troubling him but he addressed her as 'sweetheart', and signed himself, 'Your assured loving husband'. He died the day he wrote the letter. Her marital experience had been not unlike that of her mother.

She caught the smallpox from her daughter, as we have noted earlier, and narrowly escaped death, as she believed. The disease did so martyr her face that it confirmed her more and more in her mind never to marry again. From those words we may infer that Lady Anne was not ruling out the possibility of a second marriage. Very few widows in the seventeenth century overlooked that possibility; few stayed unmarried.

During her widowhood her elder daughter, 'the child', Lady Margaret, was married at the age of fifteen to John, Lord Tufton, a young man of twenty. Within two years after her marriage Lady Margaret could call herself Countess of Thanet, and the marriage proved a happy one. Lord Thanet was a good-natured and devoted husband who seems to have been fond of his mother-in-law. Of the twelve children of the union eleven grew up, six sons and five daughters, a remarkable record for that time.

Lady Anne might have remained alone. But it was a man's

world and she was in pursuit of a man's inheritance. In her difficulties an influential husband might prove useful. The man she selected was a great figure in his way but no match for her in character. Philip Herbert, Earl of Montgomery and of Pembroke, came from one of the most illustrious families in England but he was chiefly interested in horses and dogs. In tournaments and at the cockpit he was to be reckoned with, as Herberts before him.

Lady Anne had known him for a long while. She and he had performed together in at least one masque, when he was Earl of Montgomery and had not yet become Earl of Pembroke. The two must often have run into one another at Court. Philip Herbert could not but know all about Lady Anne's famous dispute over her lands. He had indeed been present, it will be recalled, on that memorable day in January of 1617 when the young Countess of Dorset had stood up to the King and to the men around him. Since then his wife and her husband had died.

He was not exactly the type Lady Anne had had in her mind's eye for a mate. Her long-time secretary had heard her declare that if God ordained a second marriage for her, she was resolved never to have a husband that had children by an earlier marriage, nor one that was a courtier, a curser, or swearer. It was her fortune, remarked Sedgewick, to light upon a husband with all those disqualifications. He had others. He was a spendthrift, like her first husband. Lady Anne's comment that he was no scholar was an understatement. Sedgewick said that he could scarce read or write. Certain it is that books, which meant much to Lady Anne, were not his hobby.

Why did she tie herself up to such a man? It is probable that the exalted position of the Herbert family was what counted with her. He was, she wrote, one of the greatest and noblest subjects of the kingdom. At another time she referred to the storms of fortune which were seldom avoided by 'those greatly born and matched'. It was her destiny to be so matched whatever happened. Finally rank was in her blood. A Clifford could not ally herself with some worthy country gentleman or with any run-of-the-mill nobleman. With her it was a consort of famous lineage or none.

Why did he marry her? She was known to have a will of her own and such ladies were seldom sought after. Could it be that her decisiveness caught the fancy of a man of his quicksilver temperament? More probably her jointure of £3400 a year interested him. He was himself a rich man but his spending was on a great scale, and he could do with more.

At first the marriage seemed to go well enough. Lady Anne, although she was forty when she married him, bore him two sons, both of whom, however, died prematurely. She managed moreover to get along fairly well with Pembroke's seven surviving children by his first marriage. He did his part: he showed sympathy for her claims to the lands in the North.

It is true that she did not find it easy to get money from him for her expenses. But 'Coz. Russel' (the fourth Earl of Bedford), who had always been her friend, pushed Pembroke into making a favourable settlement upon his wife; she was given certain lands in Kent, a release of his rights to her estates in Westmorland, and £5000 out of Craven in Yorkshire for the portion of her second daughter, Isabella.

Little happiness developed, however, between Lady Anne and her new husband, and within four years much unhappiness. George Sedgewick, who had known her almost from her youth, wrote that while the Earl was temperate in most respects he was much given to women, which caused a separation between him and the virtuous Lady Anne. Other differences arose. Pembroke wished to marry one of his sons by his first marriage to Lady Anne's second daughter, Isabella. Lady Isabella did not warm to the plan and her mother was blamed by the Earl.

The Earl's growing displays of temper could not have been

agreeable to his wife. He quarrelled with men around the Court, he set Archbishop Laud and the Queen, Henrietta Maria, against him. Even King Charles, who had bestowed many honours upon him, ceased at length to favour him. It was whispered that he was mad.

Lady Anne tells us that while at Wilton (as well as at Knole), she gave herself up wholly to retiredness and made good books and virtuous thoughts her companions. In looking back she remarked:

> The marble pillars of Knole in Kent and of Wilton in Wiltshire were to me oftentimes but the gay arbours of anguish.

By that time Lady Anne must have realized that marriage into great houses cost much in expense of spirit. In 1638 she wrote to her cousin, Russell, a letter which reveals much:

> I dare not venture to come [to London] without his leave, lest he take that occasion to turn me out of this house, as he did out of Whitehall, and then I shall not know where to put my head.

Those words might mean that the Earl had instigated the informal separation which seems to have taken place in 1634. After that date Lady Anne divided her time between Wilton, Ramsbury (near Stonehenge), a smaller Herbert house, and Baynard's Castle in London, a town house of the family. It seems that when the Civil Wars 'grew hot' she and her husband came together. But even during those uncertain days she was living much of her time at Baynard's Castle and her husband was at his usual place, the Cockpit over against Whitehall.

Fortune had dealt Lady Anne bad hands but was now to bestow upon her one wholly to her liking. In January 1641 her uncle Francis, Earl of Cumberland, died at eighty-two and was succeeded by his only son, Henry, who died two years later, leaving only one child, a daughter, Elizabeth (later to marry the elder brother of Sir Robert Boyle and become the Countess of Cork). To her the northern estates could not pass. Lady Anne's father had stated in his will that if the line of the Earl of Cumberland failed of male heirs the lands should revert to his daughter. Lady Anne came at last into those great properties in the North for which she had been striving for thirty-eight years. Her ship had come into harbour.

At this point the Earl of Pembroke was probably of advantage to his wife; he had influence with the parliamentary party. Had Lady Anne with her known royalist sympathies been alone, the parliamentary party would almost certainly have compelled her to pay heavy fines on her land for 'malignancy' and those fines might have compelled her to sell some of them. She continued in the South for six years. In 1649 she took her last leave of her husband at the Cockpit in Whitehall and set out for her northern estates. It was some months after she had been in the North that she learned of his death, from a fever.

By easy stages she travelled northward and arrived at Skipton Castle in Craven on July 18th, 1649, to find only the long gallery of the castle habitable. From one of her castles to another she moved and found them all in a poor state, Skipton being rather better provided than the rest. There she settled down, 'the first time that I lay a twelfthmonth together in any of my own houses'. At once she undertook a long programme of improvements.

She was fifty-nine years old. Instead of the frustrated existence she had led she was now to develop a continuous occupation. Those who in their late fifties start a new life and make a success of it are not too common. The dowager Countess of Pembroke had plans in which she was so interested that she was indeed another woman. Gone was the languid mistress of Knole, gone the great lady of London restlessly proceeding from one party to another, gone too the bored wife who lay abed twelve hours for want of something to do. She had now quite enough to occupy her. She wrote:

> A wise body ought to make their own home the places of self-fruition.

What she needed was a full-time job that called for the best of her mind and gave her the satisfaction of making plans and carrying them out, and her words about self-fruition suggest that she knew as much. Her mother's people, the Russells, had always been planning and putting through. She had not a little imagination of her own special kind but had never had the opportunity to give it play. In the world around us today we meet with talented women who have to spend their days in routines that become drudgery. Such unhappy creatures may find their outlets in charities, or in bridge, or in giving dinners, but now and then they suffer deeply from the want of a purposive and thus an interesting life, and break down nervously. I am inclined to suspect that Lady Anne was such a woman in an earlier generation and that more than once she had been on the edge of a nervous collapse. Nervous prostration, an illness allowed the well-to-do in our day, was unknown in the early seventeenth century, but women had spells of weeping and melancholia not unlike it.

No longer was she in danger of that. She had found her thing to do. Five castles, two of them long in ruins, three of them needing elaborate restoration, were hers to restore as liveable homes, enough opportunity for self-fruition. A sixteenth-century woman by birth, she was used to a feudal setting and castles were the outward symbol of what she knew and revered most. She set to work to bring order out of the chaos that existed throughout her possessions. In 1651 she caused the boundaries to be redrawn and then proceeded to repair her chief residence, Skipton Castle, much of which was a rubbish heap. At Appleby repairs were begun in the same year. Within eleven years that castle was in good shape. The restoration of Brough Castle started early. It had been burned a century and a half earlier. Brougham Castle was ready for occupancy a couple of years after Brough. Pendragon had been a ruin for over a hundred years but by 1663 Lady Anne was able to keep Christmas in it. In addition to those five castles she took possession of Barden's Tower which really belonged to her cousin, Elizabeth, daughter of the late Henry, Earl of Cumberland, and now Countess of Cork, and made many repairs there. Sedgewick says that her friends tried to dissuade her from so much building, telling her that Oliver Cromwell would order the restored castles to be pulled down. She answered that if he did not take her money and credit from her she would repair them even though they were thrown down the next day. Her words, says Sedgewick, were reported to Cromwell who remarked:

> Let her build what she will, she shall have no hindrance from me.

Wherever she made restorations she left inscriptions, sometimes stating when the work was begun and when finished, and often bearing her initials, A. P., in stone, with a quotation from Isaiah lviii, 12:

> And they that shall be of thee shall build the old waste places; thou shalt raise up the foundations of many generations, and thou shalt be called the repairer of the breach, the restorer of the paths to dwell in.

A restorer she was, as Bishop Rainbowe pointed out. 'It was perceived from the first,' wrote Bacon, 'when men would cure mortality by fame, that building was the only way.' Lady Anne was hardly as much interested in fame as in putting Clifford properties in order, but such fame as engraving in stone would secure she did not avoid. Today only Skipton and Appleby Castles remain. Brough, Brougham and Pendragon are no more than a few walls and masses of rubble in the fields; they were abandoned early in the eighteenth century. Even buildings do not cure mortality.

Her restorations are said to have cost Lady Anne £40,000 and must have strained her resources. To get money enough for her journey north she had to borrow £100 from a friend, which she paid back in less than a year. She had received two jointures and presently she received her legacy of £15,000. But I suspect that most of the money Lady Anne laid out for building came from what she saved from the rents of her lands.

Her dealings with her tenants were characteristic. Throughout the vicissitudes of her struggles for the Clifford lands she had kept up a tenuous connection with them. But they were canny northerners and had taken advantage of the demoralization of the Civil Wars, and quite naturally, for they had suffered losses themselves. Lady Anne understood that the condition of the country called for leniency and she made a promise:

> If I can avoid it by gentle and fair means I will not begin to use rough courses towards my tenants there, for you know how much I love that country.

Gentle means were not enough. The tenants asserted that her stewards had taken away some of their cattle. They believed that certain allowances authorized by parliament should be granted to them. In 1650 Commissioners were appointed to settle the disputes. Lady Anne began suits, meantime ejecting certain tenants. Her estate agents were reluctant to push matters and Lady Anne wrote importunate letters to Christopher Marsh, her agent, and told him:

> If you should be pinching or sparing of costs in this law suit of mine against my tenants here, you might therein do me much harm.

He expostulated with her and she wrote sharply to him. Lawsuits she disliked as much as anyone but was intent upon maintaining the rights of the Cliffords. Like her mother she was conciliatory but firm. In November 1650 the Commission set up to hear the evidence gave an award to Lady Anne and she was left to her own proceedings. It was not until 1656 that she finally won all her suits against her tenants. In the meantime she was engaged in increasing the rents.

Her secretary tells the story of the disputed hen. It was a feudal right of the owner of Skipton Castle to receive eight hundred 'boon' hens a year, one of those rare manorial rights left over from medieval times. Murgatroyd, a rich clothier of Halifax who had bought some land near Skipton, owed one hen a year to Lady Anne. He refused to pay it. Sedgewick says that the Lady Anne spent £200 at law in recovering the hen. He does not tell us the sequel of the story, which rests only on tradition, that after she had won her suit and collected the hen she invited Murgatroyd to dinner and served it as the *pièce de résistance*. The story may or may not be true, but it fits in nicely with the character of Lady Anne. Her motto was: 'Preserve your loyalty, defend your right.' Once assured of her rights she could be gracious.

A feudal life in the North was what the Countess had been born for. 'I do more and more fall in love with the contentments and innocent pleasures of a country life', she wrote, and quoted the psalm: 'The lot is fallen into me in a pleasant place, I have a fair heritage.' The lines of Samuel Daniel came into her mind:

> From many noble progenitors I hold
> Transmitted lands, castles, and honours which they sway'd of old.

She was urged to visit the Court in London and glut her eyes with the sights of gallantry and glory; her answer was that she would only consent to do so if she were allowed to go wearing blinkers, lest she should censure that which she was not able to judge competently and be offended or give cause of offence to others. She spoke as one mellowed by years and good fortune. She was apparently not disturbed by the rumours of the goings-on at the Merry Monarch's Court.

Her feudal existence involved contact with many kinds of people. Nothing is more evident from Bishop Rainbowe's discriminating account of her than that she loved to talk and did talk well. She was no elderly egoist, such as her fortune and experience might have made her. She fitted her conversation to people and their circumstances, as the best talkers do. Her words were 'pleasant or grave, always seasoned with salt, savoury, but never bitter'. With her servants she was likely to say something 'of remark', some comment perhaps on living which they would remember. She had read so much and known such good company that she must have had many stories to tell and many sayings to quote. The Bishop tells us that an eminent divine, who has been almost certainly identified as John Donne, declared that Lady Anne 'knew well how to discourse of all things from predestination to slea-silk'. That evidence of her conversational versatility comes from the days of her youth but there is reason to believe that she did not lose the talent in her assured later years.

The Bishop tells us that she avoided censorious talk which she regarded as the result of the tyranny of fashion and custom. What I suspect that she meant was that people praised the great and those in favour and took out their spites on the less fortunate. In her youth she may have observed some of the invisible control that a Court exercises on conversation. Now in her later life she was far from courts and could say what she pleased, but avoided nevertheless censorious talk whether about the great or the less important. She was willing to allow a certain latitude in judging others, especially 'public persons or actions of state', where the reasons for action were often secret.

She spent much time in thinking. She used to chew the cud, ruminating on next day's business in her night wakings. When once she had weighed the circumstances and come to a resolution she wished no reconsideration. During her wakeful hours in the night she had learned much, how to live within her means and yet carry out her plans.[1]

Through the seventy pages of his sermon about her, Bishop Rainbowe rang the changes on the theme that Lady Anne had disciplined her body and mind. In that respect how different she was from that wild bird of plumage, her father. One suspects that her capacity for discipline derived from her Russell ancestry and no doubt in part from her experiences as a young married woman.

A reader she had been from her youth. After she had gone north and was worrying about her problems with her tenantry she wrote:

> If I had not excellent Chaucer's book here to comfort me, I were in a pitiful case, having so many troubles as I have here; but when I read in that I scorn and make light of them all, and a little part of his bounteous spirit infuses itself in me.[2]

Classical authors abounded in her library: Epictetus, Plutarch

[1] All this we learn from the Bishop, with whom Lady Anne was evidently on intimate terms.

[2] She might have gone to Shakespeare for comfort — she never mentions him — but why to Chaucer? What was it in Chaucer that comforted her? Was it his humour? I cannot make out that Lady Anne had any capacity to laugh at herself or at others, unless the unauthenticated story of the hen reveals humour. Was it Chaucer's catholicity of outlook, his wide human sympathies that appealed to her? She herself enjoyed many kinds of people and may have found in Chaucer characters that reminded her of those she had known.

She loved to compare things past and present. Chaucer's pictures of an earlier century may have interested her and the historical outlook she gained therefrom may have been an influence in comforting her about the ills of the world.

(both the *Lives* and the *Morals*), Ovid, Antoninus (*Meditations*), and Ammianus Marcellinus. Once when her harassed steward, Christopher Marsh, in a letter to her quoted from the ancients, she answered that she was grateful for his sayings out of Antoninus and Seneca. Seneca would indeed have pleased her. Short, sharp, sententious comments on the conduct of living were to her taste.

She read authors of her own time: Joseph Hall, Ben Jonson, Sir Henry Wotton (*Elements of Architecture*), Guiccardini's *History* and Gerard's *Herball*, as well as many religious books. George Herbert's writings were on her shelves; she had been on friendly terms with him when she lived at Wilton and he near by at Bemerton. One of the books of Henry More, the Platonist, was in her library.

Lady Anne was always on the move from one of her castles to another, at great expense and with great effort, as if to look out from other windows. Again and again she mentioned the fact that her chamber in Pendragon Castle looked to the west and south, as if she enjoyed the declining sun. Her journeys were made with feudal pomp, almost like royal progresses. She herself rode in a coach with her two gentlewomen and maid-servants, or in a horse-litter by herself, her maid-servants in a coach, her gentlemen in a coach with six horses and her men-servants on horseback. These retainers were often the smallest part of the procession. For Lady Anne in virtue of her position in the county expected certain attentions. Important landowners such as Philip Musgrave and Sir Richard Lowther were summoned to bear attendance and some of the tenantry were expected in the procession that followed her. About the performance of these duties the neighbouring gentry and the tenantry may have been a little fretful, as belonging to an earlier generation. Other customs, now somewhat out of date, were observed: as the great lady approached the castle where she was about to stop, the church bells would ring out and she would later reward the ringers. After a fatiguing journey she would receive in the castle those who had accompanied her, give the men her hand to kiss, kiss the women and then dismiss them all. The routine of playing the great lady never palled on her.

On her journeys she would choose the most untravelled roads in order to stop at a remote village or at a cottage on the slopes of the moors. In such lonely places she liked to distribute her bounty. 'If she found not mines in these mountains,' says our friend the Bishop, 'the poor found money in good plenty.'

Those dangerous roads over the moors she seemed to prefer, wishing to go where no one had ventured before. In a coach she was pulled over roads that one would hesitate to traverse today in a car with good brakes. It must be that she delighted in the shapes of the moors, in their shoulders and backbones. It would appear that the sharp edges of the roads had no terrors for her.

She liked to come to a stop and gaze at places connected with traditions, or with her own life, or with the long story of the Cliffords. The Hart's Horn Tree in Whinfield Forest was a favourite with her. In 1333, more than three centuries earlier, one of the Balliols down from Scotland had joined with the Cliffords in the pursuit of a hart and after a long chase had caught it and nailed its horns to the tree. They had become imbedded in the tree. One horn was destroyed in 1648 and ten years later Lady Anne records the loss of the other,

> whereby we see that time brings to forgetfulness many memorable things in this world, be they never so carefully preserved, for this tree with the hart's horn in it was a thing of much note in these parts.

Even after the horns had disappeared Lady Anne continued to visit the tree and to stop a few minutes and meditate on the transitoriness of landmarks. In such spots and in others, Gillian's Tower, Wildboarfell, Hugh Morvill's Seat and The Three Brothers' Tree, she was interested — she was a sentimental old historian — and expected all her guests and relatives, when they came to visit her, to be equally interested, and to make the rounds of the several memorable sights.

Lady Anne did not neglect that hospitality characteristic of the Elizabethan times in which she had been brought up. Bishop Rainbowe tells us that the whole country was in a sense her home. Many came to see her. Already in 1651 she was entertaining her cousin, Elizabeth, the Countess of Cork, whose Barden Tower she had taken over for herself. 'There were divers differences then on foot betwixt us,' admitted Lady Anne, 'but we passed them by.' It is usually harder for those in the wrong to forgive than for those wronged, but Lady Anne was sure she was in the right. An old tower that needed reparation was of course hers. Some mead of praise is due to Lady Cork who could overlook her cousin's seizure of her tower. Lady Anne would not have been so magnanimous.

Lady Anne received others. Great nobles who were her neighbours or who happened to be in that part of the country, many of them related to her in one way or another, looked her up and stayed a day or two with her. She could be trusted to know just exactly in what degree of relationship they stood to her and she was careful to arrange that each of them should be put in a room where one of their relatives had once slept. The neighbouring gentry were in and out of her castles. The great judges coming to hold the assizes were assigned rooms, perhaps high in Caesar's Tower, or where judges had slept in other years.

Her hospitality was at its best when her offspring were involved. Her daughters, the Countess of Thanet and the Countess of Northampton, and their children came to visit her and were received with due displays of affection. In her daybook she would set down in what room each had been lodged and would call to mind who else had slept in that room and under what circumstances. Although the arrangement of guests in rooms was of her own planning she seemed to find coincidences in remembering that in the room in which her granddaughters slept, their great grandfather, her father, had been born, or died.

She received news from the outside world with little comment unless it touched her personally or her family or its history. She noted the coronation of Charles II and the arrival later of Catharine of Braganza to be his Queen, as well as the visits of William of Orange to England in 1670. The Great Plague of 1666 she barely mentioned; the Great Fire was more important since it had destroyed houses in London in which she or her relatives or ancestors had once lived.

Concerning the coronation of Charles II she was brief. From Thomas Machall's account of the celebration at Appleby on that occasion we catch a pleasant glimpse of the great lady. At each end of the town had been erected a scaffolding covered with gilded curtains. After a service at the church the Countess with the Mayor, the aldermen and many of the gentry of the country around processed through the town, with trumpets blowing and a crown carried before them, to one of the scaffolds and there fell on their knees and prayed for the King and then drank his health, 'the aged Countess seeming young again to grace the solemnity'.

At one time in her old age she found herself in touch with national affairs, and that was in connection with a parliamentary election at Appleby. When a vacancy occurred in the representation of Appleby in 1668 Joseph Williamson, who had become private secretary to the Secretary of State, the Earl of Arlington, and who was Cumberland-born, aspired to the seat. He happened to have a friend, Dr. Smith of Durham, who was a brother of the Mayor of Appleby, and the Mayor was willing to help Williamson. Lady Anne learned quickly, however, what was likely to happen, and wrote to the Mayor and Corporation of Appleby to withhold their nomination of a candidate until they heard from her. Williamson had word of Lady Anne's letter and wrote her directly, soliciting her support. Lady Anne replied in friendly terms but explained that she had plans to give the vacancy to one of her relatives. Meanwhile she sent off a letter to her daughter, Lady Thanet,[1] asking her to ascertain which one of her three sons would care to be elected for Appleby.

Shortly Lady Anne began to feel pressure upon her from various local people; indeed she was overwhelmed with letters in support of the local boy who had made good in London. The Earl of Arlington, his Majesty's Secretary of State, entered the picture and wrote Lady Anne a long and persuasive epistle in favour of Williamson:

> I would desire, and he very humbly seeks it, that he may owe this obligation . . . to your Ladyship's good graces.

The dowager Countess of Pembroke and Dorset took her time to answer and her letter was a pleasantly worded negative. She knew very well, she said, how powerful a man a Secretary of State was, and hence she was confident he could find Williamson another seat.

Meanwhile the grandsons had been talking over the request of the elderly lady and had decided that Lord Thomas should be the candidate for Appleby. At the instance of Arlington, Lord Thomas was sounded out about withdrawing. Meanwhile, however, Lord Thomas had heard from his grandmother and had been told that if he withdrew he would lose her favour. Arlington was informed that Lord Thomas did not wish to antagonize his grandmother. The Tuftons were afraid of her, the Corpora-

[1] Her daughter, Lady Thanet, had on an earlier occasion gladly accepted the 'command' of her mother, and we may suspect that the whole connection regarded Lady Anne as the head, so to speak, of the clan.

tion of Appleby was afraid of her, even her deputy sheriff, Thomas Gabetis, who would have been pleased to meet the wishes of the powers in London, was unwilling to cross her.

George Williamson wrote to his brother, Joseph:

> They have left no stone unturned for you with the old woman . . . but all to no purpose, for she is resolved wholly to stand for her grandchildren . . . there is no good to be done with an old woman.

She was as benevolent as she was domineering. Her mother had established an almshouse for poor women at Beamsley near Skipton, an almshouse still in existence, and Lady Anne kept in touch with it. Then in 1650 almost as soon as she had made herself at home in the North she set up an almshouse in Appleby which provided thirteen poor women with food and lodgings, gardens, flowerbeds and a washhouse. She visited the almshouse and expected her relatives whenever they came to see her to do the same; she would take meals with the women; she would bestow upon them little extras and invite them up to the castle for a dinner. She could be kind to them and then suddenly give them a piece of her mind. Dorothy Wilber brought up some of the bonelace which the women had made.

> I had her into my chamber and saw her paid for five dozen yards of bonelace, but I was very angry with her for bringing me so much, and I told her I would have no more of her.

Many charities she had. She sent boys to the university, she pensioned clergymen, she married off a bastard daughter of her first husband to a clergyman and assigned the bride a portion.

She made many contributions. When asked to help out the King she sent £400. She built a grammar school and gave an endowment for a moot hall in Appleby and for keeping in repair the bridge at Appleby. She took down and rebuilt several churches that had been in decay.

Her openhandedness to individuals amazes one. From three brief account books left we get some clue to her generosity. To those who rendered her some small service she would give five or ten shillings, occasionally more. Two Italian mountebanks who entertained her in her castle received a pound apiece. She gave ten shillings to some tumblers who came and amused her. The man who brought a letter from her daughter was given three pounds, and that at a time when she was paying nine shillings for the material for two dresses for herself. The New Year's presents to her servants were sometimes twice their annual wages. Lady Anne's tips were entirely out of scale with those usually given at the time. Bishop Rainbowe declared that Lady Anne was so bountiful to servants that they could afford to clothe themselves in such garb as best became the servants of so good and great a mistress.

The mistress lived simply herself. She was clad more coarsely than most of her servants. Bishop Rainbowe mentions the plainness of her chamber and furniture and contrasts the 'meanness' of her apartments with the gorgeous rooms of 'the great ones of these times'. He tells us further that her diet was sparing. His testimony carries weight, for he was one who denied himself in order to help the poor. It is borne out by what her secretary wrote of her.

Giving presents was her hobby. She would purchase fifty books of devotion at one time to give away. She would buy linen, silverware and men's and women's gloves in quantity of which to make gifts. She did not always, suggested the Bishop, take the greatest pains to consider whether the presents fitted the person.

She was not averse to receiving presents herself, as the neighbouring gentry discovered. They brought her raspberries, apples, plums and quinces from which she would make preserves. She had a weakness for 'apricocks' and her acquaintances bestowed them upon her in quantities.

Something of Lady Anne's housekeeping appears from the account books. Her household seems to have depended largely upon food from her own lands, as medieval lords had done but as few country families did in the seventeenth century. She bought some mutton but little beef or poultry and we may assume that the beef came from her own cattle and her chickens as feudal dues from her tenants. Her fish were no doubt caught and supplied by her own servants as well as her venison, of which she used much. Rabbits were an important article of the diet of her household. She bought the food for her cat. The tobacco she purchased, probably for her own pipe, came from Virginia but was sold locally. Her wine bill was large. This and that wine she made trial of, perhaps for the members of her household and for her guests. Her coal came from her own pits on Stainmoor. What articles she had to buy she procured in towns near by, even her clothes. It was her fixed policy to patronize home shops.

A portrait of her when she was over seventy makes her seem years younger and shows her in a garb and mien not unlike that of a benevolent Puritan divine. Her face might be that of a man, of an experienced and wise man, not yet feeling his years. Men and women as they grow old tend to look more alike. Her black hair falling simply frames a resolute and composed countenance of one who had known country contentments. Her eyes still start from her head but they are the eyes of one who had been granted what she asked of life. Her white collar and plain black dress bear out what people said of the simplicity of her clothes. Bishop Rainbowe spoke of the black serge she wore as 'not disliked by any and yet imitated by none'. She had won to that serenity to which many good old women attain and but few old men.

The years crept up on Lady Anne slowly as if reluctant to

approach so indomitable a lady. She made few concessions to age. In her eighty-fourth year she planned a journey from her castle at Appleby to her castle at Brougham. It was a frosty January morning. She walked through the drawing-room of Appleby Castle into the chapel, but was there seized with a 'swounding fit', or faint. After she had been carried into a nearby chamber she presently recovered herself. She got up, passed down the stairs through the hall into the court, only to faint a second time and be carried back. Her attendants tried to persuade her to return to her chamber and not to venture forth on so sharp a day. But she was not to be subdued by her body. She records what happened after her second fainting spell:

> Having also by God's blessing got well past it, I went down again into the court where I took my horse-litter.

Escorted by her retainers she made her way over rough roads to arrive safe at Brougham about four that afternoon. There she had a third attack, which she fails to mention in her diary. Her servants told her that such spells were dangerous and she answered in words that remind us of those of Sir Humphrey Gilbert a century earlier. She knew, she said, that she must die, and it was the same thing to her to die in the way as in her bed.

It is a piece of luck that the daybook for the last three months of her life, from January to March 1676, is still in existence and has been printed by Williamson. There the familiar characteristics appear, subdued possibly but not changed by weakness. Lady Anne is settling her household troubles, dealing with her stewards about the rents and putting one of them up for the night in the Baron's Chamber and another in the Musty Chamber, arranging to have her two farmers and the parson at dinner in the Painted Chamber, receiving guests and presenting them with buckskin gloves or money, sending off letters, reading the gazettes from London, rating a vintner about his expensive sack and recording gleefully: 'And then he slipped away from me in a good hurry.' Even small episodes were worth mention: her black-spotted bitch pupped in her bed.

Her chamber had become a shrine where visitors, high and low, presented themselves for what they must have realized might be the last time. She had no opportunity to become lonely; her officials still came to her for orders; her chaplain held services in her room almost constantly. She was reading the Old Testament; the Psalms and Ecclesiastes were her favourite books. The twenty-third psalm seemed to comfort her. More than once she alluded to the heathen god, Baal, and one suspects from her questions about him that she identified him with her enemies of old.

There appears a new note in her diary: 'I went not out of my chamber today.' And always after the record of a visit follows: 'And then he went away.' Did she dread to see people go, lest she might not see them again? Then she would set down: 'One or two very ill fits.' But she would add: 'Yet I slept well in the night, thank God.' She had her hair clipped and burned in the fire. She took a footbath, 'wherein beef had been boiled and bran'.

As Lady Anne approached the end of her pilgrimage, she turned, as she had doubtless done often before, to her diaries of her earlier years.[1] She seemed always to find such drama as she needed in retrospect. She was indulging herself in flashbacks. On January 19th, 1676, she looked into her diary of fifty-nine years before. On that day in 1617 the Queen (Anne of Denmark) had sent for her and advised her to persist in her refusal to trust her cause to the King and next day she had given the King an absolute refusal.

On January 25th she looked into her diary of fifty-two

[1] She does not say that she looked into her diaries but she could not have recalled the exact details and dates unless she had refreshed her memory from them.

years before to find the anniversary of the day when she and her husband dining at Knole had a great falling out. Those quarrels with her first husband had bitten deep into her memory.

On February 17th she looked into her diary of sixty years before (we can examine that diary in print). That afternoon George Abbot, Archbishop of Canterbury, and many others, had tried to persuade her by fair words and threatenings to stand by the award to be rendered by the four judges.

It had been agreed that she should go north and consult her mother, an expedient no doubt to gain time. That trip sixty years earlier she follows day by day in her record. Her husband had accompanied her part of the way. She traces the stages northward, where they stopped at night and how far they went each day.

She turned to earlier daybooks and looked up March 6th, sixty-seven years before. That was the very day when her mother had escorted her from her home in Austin Friars to the court of Little Dorset House, 'to live there with my first lord, being but married to him the twenty-fifth of the month before'. That was her last entry. Even looking into old daybooks was becoming a burden.

On March 19th, 1676, she grew ill indeed but left records for the next two days, the 21st having only one sentence:

I went not out all this day.

The next day she failed more rapidly, replying, however, staunchly to each inquiry:

I thank God I am very well.

Those were said to be her last words. That day was the end. She died in the same room in which her father had been born and in which later her mother had died, and no doubt she had so planned it.

Her funeral was held on April 14th at Appleby and her body placed in the tomb she had built for herself next to that of her mother. Her life had been satisfying as soon as she had been able to control it, as soon as she had done with husbands. Her funeral would have met with her approbation. John Tufton, her favourite grandson, was chief mourner. Edward Rainbowe, Bishop of Carlisle, the recipient of many kindnesses at her hands, preached a three-hour sermon. Lady Anne would have been pleased at the attendance at her obsequies, a vast throng, 'all her neighbours, and almost every landowner in Westmorland and Cumberland, either being present in person or represented'. It was said that all her tenantry were in attendance and some of them had come from afar. Her epitaph which she herself no doubt prepared said that 'she ceased Christianly, willingly and quietly'. The first two adverbs she had used in describing the departure of her mother. Her epitaph is to be seen in Appleby church but what is more significant is that the memory of 'Lady Anne' lingers still in her countryside.

JOHN TAYLOR

JOHN TAYLOR

TO view England through John Taylor's eyes is to look out on a world he would have called a gallimaufry. It was a jumble of many scenes, of shouting Shrovetide mobs in the City and quiet men chatting in Yorkshire alehouses: of processions along Fleet Street and deserted pavements in a cathedral town; of newsmongers in ordinaries and barbers' shops; of Cornish villagers, curious and suspicious, gathering about a stranger; of friendly and unfriendly mayors and of officious constables.

John Taylor had begun work as a waterman in London and among his fellows – drovers, cooks, bakers and artisans of many kinds – he was at home. But he looked for a better job, fancying himself as a poet, transformed himself into a traveller-to-order and a rhymer of sorts, and found himself at length the spoiled guest of gentlemen and magistrates. There were indeed few types of men with whom in his sojournings he did not develop acquaintance. He was perhaps least drawn to the middle classes; he had few good words for merchants and their retainers; he did not think well of tradesmen. They were likely to be 'sectaries', that is, Puritans, and against them he had a prejudice.

His prejudices were many and they happened to be those of not a few Englishmen of his time. He is not the less useful to us on that account. The common man of the early seventeenth century is one of whom we know little and about whom we are thus most curious. His outlook on politics and religion, his attitudes towards his betters, his occasions of amusement and indignation, his hopes and fears, however hard to discover, are as interesting as the thoughts and deeds of those in Whitehall and at Westminster.

Taylor was born in 1580 and died in 1653. The son of a chirurgeon in Gloucester, he went to school there and picked up a little Latin, but was soon off to London to learn the trade of waterman, that is, of those who ferried the public of London up and down and across the river Thames.

As a waterman he had enrolled with others in the Royal Navy. He served (when he was eighteen) in the Cadiz expedition of 1596 headed by the Earl of Essex, and was several times in the Azores. On one of the voyages to those islands Taylor with other youths from his ship set out in a small craft to explore an island, hoping to find oranges, lemons, figs and melons. All they found was rocks with patches of heath and moss. Meanwhile a heavy wind had arisen and the ship's boat could not be used to remove them from the island. For five days the storm continued and the grounded mariners were in danger of starvation. Taylor, who had been searching for food like a hungry dog, came upon a cave where some bread had been left. Several loaves he carried away and was seen eating them by one of his companions who begged one of them from him. Soon afterwards the stranded men were rescued. But two decades later, when Taylor was telling the story to a group of men in Scotland, Sir Henry Withrington, who haled from the north of England, came forward to attest its verity and to acknowledge himself as the man who had profited from Taylor's generosity. Later Withrington presented Taylor with a bay mare.

Despite the services the watermen rendered Elizabeth they found themselves in the next reign in a hard situation. In the old days 1500 to 2000 of them would sail every summer with the fleet, receiving 9s. 4d. a month, sometimes waiting long for their pay. In the reign of James I expeditions were no longer fitted out to prey upon Spain. Meanwhile the number of watermen was increasing so that there were of those living 'by the only labour of the oar', plus their dependants, at least 40,000 people, as Taylor estimated, no doubt with exaggeration. Their position was the worse because the fares they could charge had been determined in the reign of Queen Mary and had little relation to the price of living in the time of James I. But what hit the watermen hardest was the great diminution in the number of fares. In the time of Elizabeth the players had given their performances on the southern side of the river and every day three or four thousand people would take a boat to attend the theatre. That was no longer necessary. One went to the theatre on the north side of the Thames. The watermen found much of their patronage gone and Taylor appealed to the King on their behalf. At first he had some hope that his petition might be considered, but he was too optimistic. James I was never interested in the troubles of his lowlier subjects. The trade of watermen dwindled and Taylor had already turned for support to his pen.

For such a skilled trade he had little training. But he affected to believe that he had been summoned to it, like proper poets. One night when he was sitting in a boat repeating lines about Hero and Leander the Muses called him ashore and gave him a draught of Helicon. From that time on he took pains to fit himself for the career that had been marked out for him. He read Virgil, Ovid, Philotas, Godfrey of Boulogne, Chaucer, Spenser and many others. What he read he endeavoured to keep in mind, memorizing many poems. Of course he could not read Latin but he could obtain translations of Latin works. During the plague of 1625 he left London for Oxford and is said to have had some connection with Oriel College. It was possibly his experience at this time that enabled him to strew his lines with classical allusions. Those allusions went down well with his public, which did not understand them but was flattered to be offered a little learning.

Certain principles he had about his writing, or so he believed. He was not going to put out 'profane, obscene, palpable and odious lies, or scandalous libels', hoping thus to keep within the bounds of 'good men's respect'. Yet he managed to insert a good deal that would not have been acceptable to the Victorians. He was too guarded to be concrete:

> All my taxations are in general,
> Not any personal or national.

Notwithstanding his call by the Muses to his vocation he found his new role difficult:

> Verbosity and vapour was my gains,
> And poverty the portion of my pains.

He had some facility in rhymes, though no feeling for metre or rhythm. How was he to interest people? George Wither advised him, he asserted much later, to write against the Government and noblemen and to manage in some way to be imprisoned.

> Then shall you thrive, and be as you would be;
> Your books would sell, yourself get coin and fame,
> And then (like mine) renown'd shall be your name.

It cannot be said that Taylor took the advice literally but he did not quite forget it. He developed his own technique for arousing the attention of people. He would devise an unusual programme and inform the public of it. In 1614 he challenged William Fennor, who also regarded himself as a natural poet and entertainer, to a public contest on Hope stage on the Bankside. One thousand bills advertising the event were printed at Taylor's expense and distributed. The bills drew a large and expectant audience but did not bring Taylor's opponent. The crowd shouted that they were cony-catched and cheated: they raged and laughed and swore and stamped and cursed. Taylor stood his ground but began to be pelted with clods, pieces of wood and stones. Some demanded their money back. At length Taylor succeeded in some degree in quieting them and essayed a humorous dialogue, which seems to have been tolerated. It was completely overshadowed by the next entertainment, a play by professional actors. When that was done the audience fell once more to berating Taylor. His reception distressed him but not so deeply that he could not recognize the materials at hand for a story. At once he wrote a castigation of Fennor that provoked that casual writer to reply. Attack and counter-attack made both men better known to the public.

Taylor became steadily more of a figure. He did not attack great persons, as advised, but again and again he wrote against Thomas Coryat who had some reputation for his travel narratives. His controversies with Fennor and Coryat served to increase his fame.

He had this advantage, that London was 'small townish' in its essential character; once you were talked about there you were a character to be pointed out. In a preface to one of his pamphlets he complained of the notoriety he had attained, but not without self-satisfaction:

> I am of much acquaintance and cannot pass the streets, but I am continually stayed by one or other, to know what news, so that sometimes I am four hours before I can go the length of two pair of buts . . . First John Easy takes me and holds me fast by the first half an hour; and will needs torture some news out of me from Spinola, whom I was never near by 500 miles . . . I am no sooner eased of him but Gregory Gandergoose, an alderman of Gotham, catches me by the goll [hand] demanding if Bohemia be a great town, and whether there be any meat in it.

What he wrote seemed to interest the public he sought. He was against the standard sins and in favour of the recognized virtues. He disliked the Devil and he approved of the Virgin Mary. He touched on topics of the day and related his adventures in inns and on the roads. In some verses addressed to Taylor a friend tells why he read the water-poet:

> It offers much desir'd variety,
> To pass dull hours withall; with that, affords
> Much useful matter, which, with phrase and words,
> And all the aptest ornaments of writ
> Thy pen doth furnish.

In time Taylor developed the occupation he had initiated into a routine. He would announce a proposed journey: he was going to travel from London to Edinburgh and back without a penny of money, neither borrowing nor stealing on the way; he was going to scull in a paper boat from London to Queenborough on the Kentish coast; he was to proceed through Germany to Prague, and that during the wars. As soon as he had determined his itinerary he caused to be printed bills describing the coming adventure: he urged readers to subscribe a sum of any amount they pleased, but not less than sixpence, to be paid to Taylor if the journey came off. This scheme proved rewarding. It called for no great outlay of money, and yet it appealed to the eagerness of men to share in a popular project. At the end of the trip subscribers received Taylor's account of his adventures, set forth in prose and verse, with enough flings at those he had found cause to dislike to satisfy the taste of his clientele.

A sample of the prospectus which Taylor would send out before undertaking a journey is contained in one of his later works, *Taylor's Travels: London to the Isle of Wight*. It runs:

> When John Taylor hath been from London to the Isle of Wight and returned again, and that at his return he do give or cause to be given to me, a Book or Pamphlet of true news and relations of passages at the Island, and to and fro in his journey, I do promise to give to him or his assigns the

sum of what I please in lawful money of England, provided that the said sum be not under sixpence.

The subscriber signed his name on the bill posted up and presumably Taylor went round and collected all the bills with the signatures attached. Although the subscriptions were usually satisfactory, the collection of them was another matter. Taylor was forced to hound his debtors from lodging to lodging, into the back alleys of Alsatia between Fleet Street and the river, and even into suburban villages. Indeed after he found his debtors he was sometimes defied. So great was his disgust on his return from Edinburgh, when 750 of his debtors defaulted, that he wrote a pamphlet, *A Kicksey-Winsey, or a Larry-Come-Twang*, in which all his powers of denunciation were exhibited. If the debtors did not pay up at once, he promised to bring out a new edition, wherein he would satirize, cauterize and stigmatize all the whole kennel of curs. Even more than in our time men dreaded being held up to scorn in print and often paid the money they had promised.

To travel without spending any money must have been a problem. But Taylor regarded himself as a man of letters and accepted hospitality and donations of money with no loss of self-respect. His return, an ample one in his opinion, was to mention his hosts and donors in his forthcoming poem, alluding to the quality of the hospitality and the amount of money bestowed. His fame must have become fairly widespread over the kingdom, for in many instances, as he told the story, he had only to enter a town to have hospitality thrust upon him. In other cases, however, he went to the mayor or to some leading man of the town and explained no doubt what was expected in the entertaining of so famous a man. Sometimes he was disappointed. On his way north he reached Huntingdon and lodged at the home of the postmaster, at the sign of the Crown. The postmaster and innkeeper was informed, probably by Taylor's servant, of the character of Taylor's penniless pilgrimage, but he was a man of guile. He came to Taylor's chamber, and called for three quarts of wine and four jugs of beer and supped with him and his servant. It turned out that the man with Taylor had to pay the bill.

Usually the traveller fared better. When the mayor or leading townsman failed to put him up, some other citizen might come to the rescue. More often it was a country gentleman who not only took him in but kept him for several days and sent him off with a few shillings extra. Occasionally such a gentleman gave him letters of introduction to other gentlemen. It is amazing how many well-known gentlemen entertained him. Of such hosts Taylor never failed to write lines of commendation and to regard them thereafter as old friends. Even those few gentlemen who asked to have their names withheld were thanked without being named.

That Taylor was afforded such general hospitality may seem surprising. People might well have set him down as a professional 'sponge' and dismissed him. But he was an engaging personality. Aubrey wrote: 'He was very facetious and diverting company, and for stories and the lively telling of them few could outdo him.' Such a man would have been welcome in many country houses where they still offered entertainment to those who could claim some acquaintance, and often to others. Taylor had the great advantage that he had become in some slight degree a national figure and word had doubtless been passed along that country gentlemen did often entertain him. Moreover he was not wanting in self-assurance.

That is shown by his experience in Edinburgh. Having promised his public to journey to Edinburgh and to return without spending any money he arrived in that city destitute of provision or lodging for himself and for his man and horse. For a time he

JOHN TAYLOR, WATER POET

contented himself with looking at passers-by in the hope of lighting upon a familiar face. At length he grew tired of this unrewarding search. Picking upon a benevolent-looking man Taylor fixed his eye upon him and gazed seriously at him, as if tempted to speak. The man was a Scot and naturally curious about others on the street. He looked Taylor over in turn but failed to recognize him. Taylor continued his scrutiny, however, and the two approached one another, the Scot, in Taylor's words, 'much musing at my gazing, and I much gazing at his musing'. Taylor then passed on, but the startled Scot stopped Taylor's servant and asked whether Taylor was an acquaintance. Taylor's man, a fit companion for his master, denied any acquaintance but remarked that his master would be glad to meet a friend in this strange city. The explanation won over the Scot, who called Taylor to him. The two men then went off and had a drink together and proceeded to visit the show places of the town. Before the Scot had said goodbye he had lodged the traveller and his horse and servant, and lent him ten shillings.

His experiences were not always so pleasant. At an inn at Goring, where the Thames slips through the gap between the Chilterns and the Berkshire downs, the food and lodging were not so bad, but other things were:

> To bed we went in hope of rest and ease,
> But all beleaguered with an host of fleas.

At Daventry when he came to the inn he was neither invited to drink nor to spend the night. Indeed the hostess, 'having a great wart rampant on her snout', stood by in silence and watched the villagers consume a jug of beer left at the inn for Taylor's use. The water-poet took his revenge. He entreated his readers that if by chance they should come to Daventry they would 'balk' that inn. For once Taylor had gone too far. What happened we do not know, but in another pamphlet he apologized for his slur upon the Daventry hostel, since apparently the reputation of the host was better than that of his wife.

Taylor's gratitude for kind treatment was no less fully expressed. In Lancashire, where from many accounts it is evident that people were oncoming, he was warmly welcomed. At the Eagle and Child his hostess washed his shirts and bands and gave him twelve silk points as well as some bacon, and indeed, as he put it, proved a mother to him. On Master Cavill, an undersheriff, he invoked God's blessing. Sir Urian Leigh was celebrated by Taylor in forty lines as 'in every way a complete gentleman', that is, one who treated Taylor well. But he had an equally good reception in other counties. He had much to say of the jolly innkeeper, William Bradshaw, at Dover:

> A man of mettle, mark, and note, long since
> He graced was to lodge a gracious Prince.
>
> A goodly man, well-fed and corpulent,
> Filled like a bag-pudding, with good content.
>
> He is a mortal foe to Melancholy.
> Mirth is his life and trade . . .
>
> Health upon health he doubled and redoubled,
> Till his and mine and all our brains were troubled.

This stout goodfellow spoke of everyone as Jack and Tom and cousin Smith.

Taylor's trips were made in summer, usually between June and September. Some of his provision he carried with him in a knapsack. On his journey to Scotland in 1618 he listed bacon, biscuits, neat's tongue, cheese and barberries as part of his food. Usually he rode on a horse. On his trip to the Isle of Wight he travelled by coach. In his last years he walked and now and then hired a horse for short distances. When money was scarce and no inns near he had to eat under the roadside hedges while his horse fed on pulse. At times he slept in the open with rushes and ferns as his mattress. A rough way to travel it was, especially if one were plagued by rain. But sleeping outdoors on a warm summer evening was not always so bad. He had ten thousand stars overhead. Cleanliness was one of the luxuries discarded on such journeys:

> My nag through stones and dirt
> Did shift shoes twice ere I did shift one shirt.

The road was often bad:

> The clammy clay sometimes my heels would trip,
> One foot went forward, th'other back would slip.

Worst of all were the frequent arid stretches:

> My very heart with drought methought did shrink.
> I went twelve miles and no one bade me drink.

There were graver dangers than thirst unslaked. On one of his water trips, this one to York, along the east coast, Taylor and his oarsmen were forced by a storm to land at Cromer on the Norfolk shore. It was a dark night. Someone on shore raised the cry, 'Pirates!' and a tumult followed. The constables were called out and they summoned the militia. Meanwhile people for miles around, says Taylor, who was seldom given to understatement, came streaming towards the town. Taylor and his oarsmen were given no chance to explain; they were held under guard all night. In the morning two justices of the peace who had heard of Taylor accepted his story.

In all his journeys Taylor was inquisitive after novelties. At Halifax he was shown an early model of the guillotine used to behead thieves. At Hull he was impressed with the great waterworks with pipes leading into town. In the better-appointed houses it was only necessary to turn on the cock and running water flowed into the container. In Scotland he looked over the coal-mines at Cooras near Dunfermline; never had he seen any work of man to parallel them. Down into the mines he proceeded, entering by the edge of the sea and coming out by land. The mines extended for a mile beneath the sea and in most parts of them a man could walk upright. Taylor was pleased to think of the many men set at work. At Nottingham he marvelled to note how many inhabitants dwelt in vaults, holes or caves dug out of the rocks, while overhead cattle grazed and gardens were cultivated.

Taylor regarded it as part of his function to inform Londoners of the country towns. Coventry seemed to him a fair, famous, sweet and ancient city, and the strong walls about it made it unmatchable in the kingdom. Yarmouth had sumptuous and good-looking buildings and its people were industrious and courteous. As a fishing town it had no equal in England. Moreover the place had no prostitutes. Leicester met his approval. There were no schismatics, or Puritans, there. The people were so loving to one another that the lawyers wanted work. Even the few drunkards were civil and fair-conditioned. The town had a free school where instruction was given in reading English, Latin and Greek; it had a library, two jails and two houses of correction. The town took care of its poor. A hospital or bead-house lodged 110 old men,

> And nurses are allow'd to dress their meat,
> To make their beds, to wash and keep them neat.

No begging was allowed in the town and the streets were 'so clean from dunghills, filth or soil that one could walk all over the town in low shoes'.

Not all centres won such favour from the water-poet. He stopped at the Cock in Winchester. Never had he seen so few people on the streets. He walked from one end of the town to the other, and the place seemed to him dead. Did he perhaps happen on a week when the inhabitants were out in the fields working at the harvest? Salisbury made an equally bad impression. In that city were 3000 destitute people in three parishes, 'besides decayed men a great many'. But one good thing he noticed in Salisbury, a common brewhouse intended to help out the poor.

At all times Taylor enjoyed the country but in a critical year he had nothing but indignation for country people. The plague had hit London in 1625 and he had seen the city houses shut up and people dying by the hundreds, while others fled to the country. The people away from the capital were unwilling to receive anyone from the plague district. Taylor was bitter at 'those beastly, barbarous, cruel, country cannibals, whom neither entreaty of the healthy or misery of the sick could move to any spark of humanity or Christian compassion'.

In 1618 Taylor set off for Scotland, his first trip to a foreign country. He found things beyond the Border not very different:

> The hills with sheep replete, with corn the dale,
> And many a cottage yielded good Scotch ale.

Unlike other travellers to Scotland he did not complain of the dirty and wretched inns, nor did he emphasize the poverty of the country people. With Edinburgh he was charmed; the High Street was the fairest street he had seen and the squared stone buildings six or seven stories high interested him. He said nothing, however, of the romantic situation of Edinburgh, that castled rock hanging above the town, Arthur's Seat beyond Holyrood, with its natural ramparts, the wide Forth beyond which one could glimpse the kingdom of Fife. Few cities in the world are so easily and so lovingly remembered.

What annoyed him was that Edinburgh was not set close to the sea. Trade came naturally to Taylor's mind rather than far views.

The city should have been planted, Taylor wrote, a mile below on the shore, 'the sea and all navigable rivers being the chief means for the enriching of towns and cities'.

His journey to Scotland gave him a body of new experience. He was asked to go on a hunting party that included many lairds and some nobles. For a month Taylor shared a summer holiday with some of the notables of Scotland. Four days the party stayed at Ballo Castle where the quality and quantity of the food amazed the Englishman:

> Every meal four long tables furnished with all varieties, our first and second course being three-score dishes at one board; and after that always a banquet.

A smaller party, of which Taylor was one, joined that larger group of the 'nobility and gentry of the kingdom [who] for their pleasure do come into these Highland countries to hunt'. Their guides were 'Highland men who for the most part speak nothing but Irish'. Taylor was surprised to see the chief men in the strange Highland costume, but he was told that the pride of the Highlanders was so sensitive that if they felt their costume scorned they would not furnish guides or dogs. Hence Taylor put himself in that habit which he described as

> shoes with but one sole a piece, stockings . . . made of a warm stuff of divers colours, which they call tartan . . . a jerkin of the same stuff that their hose is of, their garters being bands or wreaths of hay or straw, with a plaid about their shoulders, which is a mantle of divers colours . . . with blue flat caps on their heads, a handkerchief knit with two knots about their neck.

The party made its way into the fastnesses of the Highlands and for twelve days Taylor saw neither houses nor people (except the hunters), only 'deer, wild horses, wolves, and such like creatures'.

Hunting had already become an organized sport with the maximum of pleasure and the minimum of discomfort. Between 1400 and 1500 men and their horses were employed, according to Taylor's estimates, which may always be safely cut down. Early in the morning about 500 or 600 of the guides and servants would rise to disperse through a district of seven to ten miles. Then they would herd the deer to a specified place. By that time the gentlemen would be up and waiting. Suddenly the deer would come in view over the hills, 'their heads making a shew like a wood'. Then a couple of hundred of Irish greyhounds would be loosed upon the prey. Taylor tells us that by the use of dogs, guns, arrows, dirks and daggers, eighty deer would be slain within the space of two hours.

This wholesale and manipulated sport Taylor enjoyed, whether for its own sake or because of the company into which he was thrown it is hard to say. He had come to know important people, and, as he travelled south towards the Border, he was entertained by a succession of lairds, to whom he had been given letters. These lairds won his admiration because they wore homespun clothes and were less pretentious than the English gentry. The Scottish noble, he wrote,

> never studies the consuming art of fashionless fashions, he never tries his strength to bear out four or five hundred acres on his back at once, his legs are always at liberty, not being fettered with golden garters and manacled with artificial roses.

The laird was simply attired but he would entertain for several days together a party of earls and knights and their retainers. To such feasting Taylor had no aversion.

As he left Edinburgh for the south he happened upon Ben Jonson, who gave him a piece of gold to drink his health in England. Taylor was pleased to see that his fellow countryman was being entertained among gentlemen and noblemen, as he himself had been.

Taylor did not confine himself to narratives of travel. He published verse and prose on a variety of subjects. He related the story of the downfall of Mr. Rowse who started well and went downhill until he murdered his two small children and suffered execution. Taylor drew morals from the story, one of which was that Rowse lived in a town with no preacher. Noblemen interested Taylor and on their deaths he wrote laboured elegies. He gave the public a small volume of *Wit and Mirth*, which consisted of 153 episodes, some of them stories drawn from his own experience, more of them stories in circulation at the time, and a few of them merely brief comments intended as epigrams. He wrote about Thomas Parr, a Shropshire yeoman, who was supposed to have lived to the age of 153:

> He ne'er knew history, nor in mind did keep
> Ought but the price of corn, hay, kine, or sheep.
> Day found him work and night allowed him rest.

The last line is probably the nearest to poetry of anything Taylor ever wrote. He brought out *Taylor's Pastoral* in which he talked at length of sheep and shepherds in biblical and classical times and about wool and clothmakers and said nothing interesting in any way. He wrote at length of Hempseed in which he expatiated on the value of hemp to make cloth, cordage, halters, ropes and sails. He composed long poems on the Virgin Mary and on the Siege of Jerusalem. He denounced the sin of pride in hundreds of lines and was no less in earnest about the Curse of Swearing. He published a prose piece on *A Navy of Landships* in which he treated of Scholarship, Goodfellowship, Apprenticeship, Courtship, Friendship, Fellowship, Footmanship, Horsemanship, Suretyship, Worship, Huntsmanship. It would be tiresome even to name his several works, but some of them went into a second and occasionally a third edition. He was so popular that he was imitated.

His travelling proved of use to the public. He made two guides. The first was a catalogue of inns in the ten shires near London.

> I have laid the foundations of this project myself; it is a vineyard of mine own planting, the grapes of mine own pressing, the wine of my own vintage (or vantage).

He told something of the counties, not a great deal, praised or dispraised a town, gave the origins of town names (usually traditionally and wrongly), and offered in Baedeker fashion a few historical notes. In the case of the inns he put down the names of the landlords or mistresses, and often the names of the landlords without the names of the inns.

The second of his guide-books was the *Carrier's Cosmography* (1637), a directory of carrier services from London to the country and from the country to London, arranged alphabetically by towns. The carrier service had innumerable branch offices unfortunately not co-ordinated through a central bureau. Taylor did his best to list exactly when carriers would leave for given places and from what inn, and when and at what times they arrived from various points in the country. From inn to inn he worked through London with note-book and pen in hand in order to find times and places of departure and arrival. At first he had to overcome some suspicion on the part of carriers; they did not understand his curiosity and feared lest some advantage be taken of them. But he had a way of getting round strangers and after extensive association with all sorts of carriers and innkeepers he had ready his manual of destinations, stops *en route*, junctions for transfer and so on. The carrier service was better than might be supposed. Generally the carriers left London on Thursday or Friday and arrived at their destinations in time to rest over Sunday and to return early in the week. In London they gathered at favourite inns, such as the Three Cups in Bread Street, or the Rose in Smithfield. Taylor explained, for example, that the wagons or coaches from Cambridge arrived every Thursday and Friday at the Black Bull in Bishopsgate Street. John Milton, in his poem about the carrier, Hobson, refers to that inn. He is speaking of Death which finally stopped Hobson and says:

> He [Death] had any time this ten years full
> Dodged with him betwixt Cambridge and the Bull.

So far as I can make out Taylor was able to make a living out of his writings. If anything went wrong, he once declared, he could go back to his trade of waterman; he had kept up his connection with the watermen, who were proud of his fame, and used him whenever they needed a friend at court.

He had a wife to support but had little to say about her. In his younger days, so he wrote, he had praise for her and could not dispraise her now:

> I have by my long experience found
> I had been undone, had I not been bound.
> I have my bonds of marriage long enjoyed,
> And do not wish my obligation void.

In another passage he spoke of his marriage as an equal partnership but he took pains to see that his wife did not gain the upper hand.

Taylor's later years from the beginning of the Civil Wars until his death in 1653 were less characteristic but interesting. The face of England was changed for the worse and the marks of war and anarchy were to be seen everywhere and were not glossed over by the water-poet.

In 1644 he happened to be in Maidenhead when he was accosted by three ragged soldiers of the parliamentary party. At once they relieved him of his coat and bag. But that was not quite the end of the story. Taylor joked with them until they led him into an alehouse and treated him. The three spent the evening together singing and telling stories and in the end Taylor received back his belongings.

Pamphlet after pamphlet he issued about the Civil Wars. He was particularly fond of making the Devil speak, who would praise the Parliamentary Party and the Puritans for their wonderful service on his behalf. Taylor denounced many of the parliamentary leaders by name and exulted over the death of Pym. He complained of the confiscation of the lands of the royalists and the assessments the so-called 'malignants' had to endure. That a waterman should have come to the defence of the landed class is significant of the hold that class still had upon the average man. Taylor took upon himself to answer many of the assertions made by the parliamentary newspapers of the time. He was rash enough to draw upon himself the fire of that skilful pamphleteer, William Prynne. Taylor knew nothing about the use of reasoned argument, but he could call names with the best of them:

> For if they snap at mine I have a pen
> That, like a trusty dog, shall bite again.

He could bite. He wrote how the gunsmiths, the armourers and saddlers had expressed their thankfulness for the wars started by Pym and his crew by giving them presents. In this case it was not the wicked munition-makers who started wars, but the makers of war who won appreciation from the makers of munitions. Taylor went further: 'The very whores do pray very zealously for you, for putting down the spiritual courts, by which means they are all trade free.' His opponents were probably not much concerned at his attacks, which were laboured and wanted a sense of reality.

During the early part of the Civil Wars Taylor was in Oxford where he is said to have kept an inn. He survived the siege of Oxford and went back to London in 1645 and took an alehouse there, the Crown, just off Longacre. After the King's execution he renamed his place the Mourning Crown, but when he found that title not well received he dubbed it the Poet's Head. Aubrey says that he had a picture of himself on the sign and under the picture these verses:

> There's many a head stands for a sign.
> Then, gentle reader, why not mine.

On the other side were the lines:

> Though I deserve not, I desire
> The laurel wreath, the poet's hire.

After the execution of Charles I in 1649 Taylor wrote elegies upon him and in that year was arrested for corresponding with the King's friends, but was presently released. Slowly he bowed his head to the inevitable. A faithful servant and subject he had been, he said, for forty-five years, but times had changed. Oliver Cromwell was ruling England and Taylor decided that he had best submit to the Government in power.

In the same year at the age of seventy Taylor undertook what he thought was to be his last journey over the country:

> My wit was worn threadbare, half-naked, poor,
> And I with it went wool-gathering for more.
> This long walk (first and last) I undertook
> On purpose to get money by my book.
> My friends (I know) will pay me for my pain,
> And I will never trouble them again.

It was a strange country, recovering gradually from the Civil Wars. Military law prevailed and soldiers were stationed in towns and at seaports to check the names, occupations and destinations of travellers. The Government was on the watch lest Royalists should start a rebellion.

Taylor left Abingdon, a few miles down river from Oxford, on a hired horse, for Faringdon. Faringdon had been burned by the King's party but was beginning to bud and spring up again. 'Here and there a pretty house peeps up.' When he reached Bath, the mayor, who was Lord Baron of the Brown Loaves and Master of the Rolls, that is, a baker, sent for him and entertained him most kindly 'with both hands in his pocket', and 'like a man of few words, forbore to say welcome to town'. They parted dryly; that is, Taylor was given nothing to drink. He went on to Wells, where he found that the goodliest of cathedral churches had been defaced by the soldiers.

His really unpleasant experience was at the Rose and Crown in Netherstowey. He found the hostess away and the host drunk. The inn was 'most delicately decked with exquisite, artificial, and natural sluttery, the room besprinkled and strewed with the excrements of pigs and children, the walls and ceilings adorned and hanged with rare spiders' tapestry, or cobweb lawn', and the smoke so thick that he could see nothing. The host swigged off a pot to him and bade him be merry and asked him if he would have powdered beef and carrots for supper. Taylor went out and sat in the street where his host visited him at intervals. At 7 p.m. Taylor went to see if his supper were ready but found the fire out and the host asleep. He awakened him but was told that there was no beef and was asked if he would be content with eggs fried with parsley. Taylor waited in his room till 9 p.m. and was then given only a piece of bread and butter. He went to bed and was furiously assaulted by an army of fleas. He occupied himself in squashing the fleas and was finally falling asleep when children began to cry, the dogs started barking, and the hogs made noises for their breakfast. Taylor had had enough; he got up and went on half-asleep ten miles to Dunster.

At Barnstaple he was entertained by a man who gave him 'fiddler's fare', meat, drink and money. In Cornwall the hills looked high and churlish but the people were affable and courteous. Near St. Michael's Mount he stayed for seven days with Francis Godolphin whose house was a 'stately, ancient palace'. Godolphin took him to see his tin-mines and showed him workmen engaged in the refining and melting of tin.

Taylor avoided Pendennis Castle lest he be questioned by the soldiers stationed there. At the fishing town of Mevagissey there were two taverns and six alehouses and he went the rounds looking for lodgings. Finding none he sought out a constable but to no avail. Meanwhile the people were staring at him as if he were a strange beast. Finally he went into the house where he had first demanded a room but was at once ordered away. He offered to fight a young knave who was about to throw him out, upon which the hostess promised him a bed. Just then an ancient gentleman appeared from another room, a justice of the peace, and promised that he would see the stranger lodged. Taylor was entertained by the justice and found 'more Protestant religion in two days than I had in five years before'.

From Cornwall he turned towards London, stopping at Plymouth and at Exeter. At Wilton he saw the magnificent seat of the Earl of Pembroke.

> It may be a palace for the greatest king in Christendom; the springs and fishponds, the garden, the walks, the rare artificial rocks and fountains, the ponds with fish on the house-top, the strange figures and fashions of the water-works, the . . . innumerable varieties of fruits, flowers; yea all, and everything that may make an earthly paradise is there to be seen, felt, heard, or understood.

Taylor was discouraged:

> And yet I every day must wander still
> To vent my books and gather friends' good will.

He was, he declared, following in the steps of a mighty king who marched up a hill and then marched down again.

But in 1652 he made yet another journey, in his seventy-fourth year, with the right leg going and left leg lame. Twelve journeys he had made and this, he promised, would be his last. Nearly three thousand people had agreed to pay him, some of whom actually paid in advance.

He was an old man and well known and many people at various stops entertained him or paid his reckoning and sometimes gave him money in addition. At a draper's shop in Warwick he was offered such refreshment that within five miles he fell off his horse twice. Coventry proved a dry town, but at the George at Lichfield he was well lodged and well did cup and sup. At Chester he met two brothers whom he had once known and a famous Italian physician did much for his lame leg and paid his bill at the inn.

He crossed into Wales and remarked at once the absence of what he was accustomed to expect in English villages: there was no saddler, no weaver, no brewer, no butcher or button-seller, not even an alehouse. What was worse:

> They have neither service, prayer, sermon, minister or preacher, nor any church door opened at all, so that the people do exercise and edify in the churchyard at the lawful and laudable games of trap, cat, stoolball, racket, etc.'

Here he was getting at a fundamental want in much of Wales. At Newmaris he looked up Lord Buckley but was snubbed. At Carnarvon he was summoned back by the Governor as soon as he learned who Taylor was, and used 'respectively and bountifully'. In general he had nothing to complain about in the way the Welsh treated him and received much free entertainment and some money.

In 1653, the last year of his life, when he was in his seventy-fifth year he set off on another journey, this time, he says, without any plan as to where he was going:

> That nothing now but age and want is left me,
> This makes me travel and my friends to try,
> Else I might, like my fellows, starve and die.

This time he went again, as in his earlier trips, on horseback.

Good fortune attended him. The people of Sussex proved kindly. In many places he was entertained by gentlemen and in other places where he stopped at an inn people in the community paid his reckoning. In one instance, I think, he had to pay his own bill of eighteenpence. At Petworth he was given hospitality by the Earl of Northumberland in the servants' quarters and was looked after by the cook. That he was not received personally by the Earl hurt him a little, but he was, he wrote:

> never so rude
> To flatter, fawn, or basely to intrude.

He was better treated at Tarring (which he called Torring), where the parson gave him six meals and lodged him three times. He stopped at Billingshurst, Steyning, Lewes, Battle, Pevensey, Hastings and Winchelsea and then left Sussex for Kent, proceeding as far as Gravesend and thence back to London. Several days he stayed with the High Sheriff of Sussex where he was introduced to a new and delicate dish, wheatears, a bird that appeared on the scene for six weeks in harvest and then vanished until the next harvest. The flesh of the wheatear, he said, tasted like marrow. Taylor was old and tired and he did little investigation of the villages and towns he visited, contenting himself with quoting from Camden.

Only two pamphlets in his controversial series written during the Cromwellian period are worth examination; those in which he introduces Christmas as a person. In the first, *The Complaint of*

Christmas (1646), Christmas comes to London and fails to hear the sound of a bell. In the second pamphlet, *Christmas in and Out* (1653), Christmas wanders up and down the country and is given now and then a single cup of slender, lean, small beer. Finally Christmas comes to Devon and Cornwall and was saluted with much love and courtesy:

> I was had into the parlour, there I was placed at the upper end of the table, and my company about me; we had good cheer and free welcome; we were merry without music . . . After dinner we arose from the board and sat by the fire, where the hearth was embroidered all over with roasted apples, piping hot . . . Within an hour after we went to church, where a good old minister spoke very reverently of my master, Christ . . . After prayers we returned home, where we discoursed merrily . . . Supper being ended we went to cards, some sung carols and merry songs . . . then the poor labour ing hinds and the maid servants, with the ploughboys went nimbly to dancing, the poor toiling wretches being all glad of my company . . . and therefore they leaped and skipped for joy.

It will be seen that at his waterman's best Taylor was a better than commonplace observer. In *Fair and Foul Weather* he talked of English sailors as Kipling of Tommy Atkins. The milksops presiding over tobacco shops regarded sailors as rude fellows who smelled of tar and pitch. The sailors deserved better. They had to play the man for King and country. They were the bulwarks of England against foreigners:

> Their painful toils do make great kingdoms rich.

> These men must stand to it; there's no way to fly.
> There they must as conqu'rors live or conquer'd die.

Taylor's outlook upon his world deserves examination. He was a bundle of prejudices, as we have seen, some of which were his own and others characteristic of his class. Bits of social analysis he made that, while not penetrating, were his own. He looked inquiringly into the shop window, even if he did not enter.

As might be expected, he disliked coach-makers, for coaches were filling the streets of London[1] and reducing the demand for watermen. But when he went on to contrast the position of coach-makers with that of cart-makers or wheelwrights, he had something to say. A maker of carts exercised an occupation long used and necessary. Yet cart-makers were so poor that the best of them seldom wore anything better than a calf-skin coat, nor had better food than a piece of neck beef and carrot roots for Sunday dinner. Nor did such skilled men ever attain an office better than that of a scavenger or a tithing man. Coach-makers were on another level. They had the gainfulest trade about the town; they dressed in satins and velvet, and could become vestrymen in their parishes. As for food they lived on the best with jellies and kick-shaws, baked swans, hot and cold pasties and red-deer pies.

Like many another brought up in a sparing way, Taylor was inclined to measure a man's position by the food he was able to command. His very soul was stirred by the thought of good food. He had dined often enough in country houses to have some notion of good eating. He liked a venison pasty, mutton joints, pigeon pies, chickens, capons and a mighty scarlet lobster. Lobsters, always scarlet, figured often in his lists. Such delicacies

[1] 'In the year 1564 Guilliam Boonen, a Dutchman, became the Queen's coachman, and was the first that brought the use of coaches into England.

'And after a while divers great ladies, with as great jealousy of the Queen's displeasure, made them coaches and rid in them up and down the Countries, to the great admiration of the beholders, but then by little and little they grew usual among the nobility, and others of sort, and within twenty years became a great trade of coachmaking.' Stowe, John, *Annals* (1631), p. 867. The Continuation of Stow from 1603 is by Edmund Howes. Howes has much social and economic information not readily found elsewhere and very definite. He has much to say about the Dutch immigration into England and may have been related to some of the Dutch families in London.

should be washed down with plenty of sack, claret, or beer. Other good things to eat were oysters, geese, woodcocks, custard and salmon. He knew all about what he called the English diet, Norfolk dumplings, Devonshire whitepot, Gloucestershire white puddings, Worcestershire black puddings, Shropshire pan-puddings, Somersetshire white puddings, and Hampshire hasty-puddings, by which we gather that the English were as fond of pudding in the seventeenth century as they are today. He had something to say in favour of cheese cake, flawn or fool, tansy-cake, pancakes, fritters and flapjack. Praise he gave to good housekeepers, and there were not too many:

> May England's few good housekeepers be blest
> With endless glory and eternal rest.

Good fellowship at the table and good manners in eating contributed to Taylor's happiness. He held the Germans up to scorn as silent and rapid gobblers of their food.

With good food went cleanliness and comfort. Taylor had learned to appreciate table-cloths and napkins and toothpicks. In honour of his laundress he wrote a pamphlet about clean linen, in which he discoursed of well-laundered and spotless handkerchiefs and of fresh sheets, luxuries seldom mentioned in the seventeenth century. He was happy when his shirt and bands were washed; travelling for long in dirty clothes made him uncomfortable.

His moral conceptions were probably those of the more respectable townsmen, and yet they were a little more than that, they were based somewhat on observation and experience. He was never weary of condemning swearing. Swearing unfortunately was believed to be manly, to become a gentleman, a fine embroidery of speech, like gold lace.

The chicanery of the time roused his indignation. Men made a living by swearing falsely before juries, an abuse that Taylor was one of the few to mention and condemn. He denounced the impostors who put up bills advertising quacksalver remedies, pills guaranteed to bring about quick cures. Such men picked a living out of others' dying.

About the evils of drunkenness he used many opprobrious nouns and adjectives. He was the more convincing because he could speak in praise of good ale:

> Not drunken nor sober, but neighbour to both,
> I met with a friend in Alesbury Vale.
> He saw by my face that I was in the case
> To speak no great harm of a pot of good ale.[1]

He could say more in dispraise of drinking. It was the poor who suffered most. The beggar spent his all in the alehouse in order to drive away care; he had nothing to lose. The rich man was likely to drink more moderately because he must 'bear a brain to look to what he hath'. But the rich and poor, if overcome, were treated differently. If the gallant staggered along the street men would say, the gentleman is sick, and would help him to his house. But if a porter or a carman was seen in the same condition, he would be placed in the stocks and suffer the derision of his fellows. Taylor was right. The more respectable classes were almost never set in the stocks.

From his own experience Taylor knew that it was hard to avoid drinking too much on occasion. He had suffered from the importunities of good fellows. When he dined at the board of a rich man the servants would force him afterwards to accompany them to the cellar or buttery where in the way of kindness they would make a man's belly like a sowse-tub. They would call: 'Off with your lap', 'Wind up your bottom', 'Up with your toplash'. For himself he preferred three days' fasting. Drink led to all the other evils in the world.

[1] These lines are almost too rhythmical to be of Taylor's composition. Did he insert in his poem the lines from some well-known drinking song?

The conditions in jails aroused his indignation. Both the jailor and the old prisoners collected a fee from each newcomer: the underkeeper won his master's approval only if he treated the prisoners with inhuman cruelty. Living conditions in jails were disgusting:

> Perhaps the jailor in one stinking room
> Hath six beds, for the gallant and the groom,
> In lousy linen, ragged coverlets;
> Twelve men do lodge in those six beds he sets.

Such lodging cost a groat a night, which went to the jailor. That official, who was out to make money, not only imposed upon the inmates, but did what he could to make them fear him:

> Will like a demi-devil domineer,
> Roar like a bearward, grumble, snarl, and growl.

Economic evils Taylor recognized. Usurers he deemed bad people; he had the medieval attitude towards the taking of interest. But he was more concerned with projectors and patentees. They gained patents for soap, starch, tobacco, pipes, pins, butter, wines, coals, cards, dice, etc. They had the art to cheat the commonweal and tricks to pass the seal, that is, to gain royal authority,

> Not thinking there would come a Parliament.

What a surprising admission by Taylor, that Parliament had its uses! The Crown had granted many patents that raised the price of living and Parliament had forced it to rescind a large number of them. The reference by Taylor was made in a pamphlet published in 1641, but perhaps written in the 1620s when the abuse of patents was most flagrant.

Taylor had much to say about extortioners and their wickedness but, as usual, was vague in describing their methods. Towards landlords he revealed an attitude that was common:

The landlord is a thief that racks his rents,
And mounts the price of rotten tenements,
Almost unto a damned double rate.

Taylor was more than a railer against abuses. He had his own schemes for the improvement of conditions. He knew a way to set the poor at work. He would give them jobs at cleaning and dredging the rivers. On that subject he offered his bit of historical philosophy. Towns with access to the sea directly or by river flourished, and those without such access withered up. He was for ever praising the Dutch who had developed trade by clearing up and deepening their rivers and by making canals to join rivers. He looked at his natal town of Gloucester. If the Severn could be so improved that large boats could come up to the city, eight men towing a barge could carry as much as forty carts with five horses and two men apiece could transport. Gloucester might carry on as thriving a trade as any city in the kingdom.

Taylor did what he could with those who had influence to interest them in the improvement of rivers. After he made his wherry trip from London to Christchurch on the Hampshire coast, he was persuaded by a waterman born in Salisbury to go up the river Avon from Christchurch to Salisbury 'for the discovery of the sands, flats, depths, shoals, mills and weirs which are impediments and lets'. A triumphal procession it proved. At Ringwood he was met by His Majesty's trumpeters who gave him a flourish on their trumpets. At Hale he was welcomed by the right worshipful Thomas Penruddock, who, so he was assured, would be a forward and liberal benefactor towards clearing the river. At Langford, further up the river, two miles below Salisbury, he was received by another worthy who was equally favourable.

It was about the Thames that Taylor was most concerned. As to that river he seems to have made some impression on the

Government. He was appointed by Dudley Carleton, Lord Dorchester,

> To view what wrongs the river Thames did bear.
> I served then, and every stop and weir,
> And all impediments I found I writ,
> And (hoping for amendments) printed it.

Promises, he declared, were made to him but he found not half that done which was promised. Many years later when Charles I was at Oxford during the Civil Wars and when Taylor was eager for some recognition for all the pamphlets he had written against Parliament, he won a hearing for his ideas about the Thames and was ordered by the Lords Commissioners and the King to co-operate with the water-baily in clearing the river of dead hogs, cats and carrion horses.

Taylor's religion was less important to him than to many in his time. All that he asked in the way of spiritual guidance was afforded him by the service of the Church of England. To see the national church challenged, and by the common man, went against his grain. Dissenters were, he believed, debasing the dignity of religion, making a hotchpotch of it; it had become the common discourse of every tavern and alehouse, where a man could hardly find five men of the same opinion. The Devil's agents, by which Taylor meant the Puritans, insinuated themselves among foolish women and silly tradesmen. Coachmen, carters, colliers, tinkers and tub-preachers abused the Scriptures with new interpretations and expositions. One of the ignorant preachers referred to Goliath as a minor prophet. Taylor described the plans of the Devil for new plantations in New England. A group of sectaries was awaiting ship at Yarmouth when a brother came to Howgrave's wife and told her news of a fallen sister.

Fallen (quoth she) from the Word? I hope not that. It was

explained that the sister was with child by a faithful brother. Well, well (quoth she), we all have gone aside. Such tales were circulated among those who disliked the Puritans.

His anti-Puritanism should have made him a supporter of a liberal Sunday and so he was. On a journey into the west he had come into a village where the children were not allowed to play on the Sabbath. Moreover, two women walking in the fields on Sunday afternoon were condemned to pay sixpence apiece or be laid an hour in the stocks and they chose to jest it out and lay both by the heels merrily an hour. His sympathies were with the children and the two women.

But Sabbatarianism in another form at Berwick-on-Tweed failed to excite his ridicule. It was in 1618 when Taylor was returning from Scotland that he found the inhabitants of Berwick in a desperate position. For years they had been forbidden to fish on Sunday but in the summer of Taylor's visit some had broken out and ventured to fish on that day. The results of man's disobedience were impressive. The salmon took matters into their own hands and disappeared from the river. Nine weeks had elapsed and still at the time of Taylor's visit no salmon could be found and the inhabitants of Berwick feared that they were being punished for the profanation of the Lord's Day. Taylor did not stay to find whether the salmon returned to the river.

Although Taylor had the prejudices of ordinary English people against Papists and bandied about the catchwords of anti-Christ and Jesuit, he was more nearly in sympathy with them than with the Puritan sects. He liked their affability, their learning and their charity. His veneration for the Virgin Mary and his liking for ritual would not have displeased the Catholics.

He was in many ways a typical Englishman of his class. His loyalty to the Crown, his fierce Englishry, his distrust of foreigners, his attitude towards courtiers and gallants, and towards the gentry and merchants, were what we might expect. His pride in his Sovereign was so great that in all his writings he uttered not the least criticism of James. He urged Scots and English to vie in rivalry which could be most true to his Majesty. He was naturally pleased to think that he was known to the King. Had he not presented one of his books to James? Ben Jonson tells us that King James said he had never seen any verses in England like to the sculler's, a statement we may well believe. He was as loyal to Charles I as to James. He saw nothing but good in him and alluded to 'his never broken word'. Few defenders of Charles I would go as far as that.

He had his own pride in his country and countrymen, a pride widely shared by his compatriots. He never made fun of Englishmen, although he once remarked that it was the nature of Englishmen not to know when things were well, an obvious allusion to the Great Rebellion. He liked to relate the martial achievements of his fellows, the glories of Crécy, Poitiers and Agincourt. In 1640 when an English ship manned by only a few men ran into two large Turkish vessels near the Scilly Islands and beat off the attack he rushed into print with the story. He took the kings of England in chronological order and wrote verses about them, detailing their warlike deeds and catching as little as possible of the significance of their reigns. Of the great Eliza, whom it was the fashion to eulogize, he could not say enough, and he was not given to economy of words. He boasted of England's East India merchants and, had he lived two centuries later, would have been an imperialist. That the English were more aware of foreign affairs than their continental cousins was axiomatic with him. He paid his respects to English law: 'Every honest man and true subject dares look the law in the face.'

Of course he distrusted foreigners. For the Germans with their execrable food, their bad roads and their cruel criminal law he had little good to say. As for the French he had never seen them at home, but could not take them seriously. The term Monsieur was to him one of contempt. Oddly enough he liked the Dutch, and for a special reason of his own. They did not allow their rivers to be silted up, as the English were doing. He adverted to the English commonplace that the Dutch had taught the English how to drink and swill and thought the English in that respect worse than the Dutch.

About peoples nearer home he was not uncritical. He spared the Scots, as we have seen, no doubt because he had been so well treated in their country, and because James I was Scottish. Yet when the Scots moved down into England during the Civil Wars and pushed their Presbyterian forms his enthusiasm for them was lessened. The Welsh he thought a poor lot. Of one of his travelling companions he wrote: 'I begin to suspect him to be a crafty knave . . . and inded after I had inquired what countryman he was, he told me he was a Welshman.' The Irish he disapproved of because they were Catholic. So stirred up against them was he by the Irish Rebellion that he urged that Cheapside Cross be taken down and melted into bullets to kill Irish rebels.

What did this poetaster, who shared so many of the prejudices of the common people of his time, think of the classes above his own?

Courtiers and hangers-on at Court received few good words. Their affected manners and their foreign phrases, their 'cringes, congés and courtesies', were un-English and unmanly. A casual gallant he recalled with resentment, who had once come down to the waterside, demanded a boat with two oarsmen, shouted at the oarsmen to increase their speed, and then left them without paying, fixing a rendezvous for the settlement, but never appearing. There were many such:

> One part of the gentry they will ne'er forget,
> And that is, that they ne'er will pay their debt.

Taylor had, however, no wish to alter the structure of society.

He warned the Roundheads that if they began to pull down kings they would have no lords and gentlemen left. The upper classes, he believed, had their place. The old-fashioned country gentleman offered hospitality and was on good terms with his tenants; he supported twenty or thirty servants, he fed the widows and the fatherless. Yet not all gentlemen were so worthy. As justices of the peace some of them accepted presents which were nothing less than bribes and left the real work of their offices to clerks.

Of the merchant class Taylor had little good to say. They were charitable, to be sure, and built almshouses, but they made more by extortion than they gave away.

His attitude towards his superiors in the writing craft is revealing. He thought fairly well of them, perhaps because he had received some consideration from them. Literary men can be too kind to those less talented in the use of the pen. Thomas Dekker, Samuel Rowlands and Nicholas Breton were the better known names among many who wrote verses in the front of Taylor's publications to recommend that poet to readers. He dedicated books to many important people, among them one to Ben Jonson, 'my long approved and assured good friend'. That Jonson wrote in praise of Taylor or dedicated any writing to him there is no evidence.

A time came indeed when whatever friendship Jonson felt for Taylor was put to a strain, and that was when Taylor made his pilgrimage to Edinburgh and quickly published his account of it. Jonson had previously announced his intention of making a foot journey to the northern kingdom. He did indeed go there and visited the Scottish poet and *littérateur*, William Drummond of Hawthornden. Drummond tells us that Jonson confided to him that Taylor was sent to scorn him. It is hard to believe that Jonson should have feared competition from the water-poet.

One looks for humour in the writings of Taylor. There was possibly more humour among men of his type than among those in the higher walks of life. One feels sure that the waterman, who was obviously one of the boys when the ale went round, must have had some sense of fun. His writings show a slight turn for satire:

> Shall we think the Scots are such fools, if they conquer, to return back again to their Whig [sour milk, or buttermilk, or fermented whey] and Scotch porridge, frost and snow (and little wood), from good featherbeds, gallant houses, English beef, ale, and broadcloth? No, Britannicus, if that day once come, the brotherhood shall find their brethren of Scotland will be the elders and carry away the land.

There are passages of lighter humour. In one place he is talking of the cooks in great men's houses and he characterizes them as Monarchs of the Marrow Bones, Marquesses of the Mutton, Lord High Regents of the Spit, Barons of the Gridiron, and Sole Commanders of the Frying Pan.[1] He is developing the incongruous, giving lordly titles to humble workers, a common form of Elizabethan humour.

In another pamphlet he exploits the Great Eater of Kent, Nicholas Wood, whom he had visited, hoping to persuade that famous character to come to London and under Taylor's auspices exhibit his prowess at eating. The great eater had been known to consume a whole hog at one time and then to finish off with three pecks of damson plums, or so Taylor affirmed. Other yarns about Wood's capacity Taylor related and then proceeded to gather phrase upon phrase:

> He holds fasting to be a most superstitious branch of Popery, he is a main enemy to Ember weeks, he hates Lent worse than a butcher or a Puritan, and the name of Good Friday affrights him like a bull-beggar; a long grace before

[1] He probably got this idea from Thomas Nash. See 'Pierce Penniless' (*Works*, ed. by McKerrow), I, 173.

> meat strikes him into a quotidian ague; in a word he could wish that Christmas would dwell with us all the year, or that every day was metamorphosed into Shrove Tuesday.

Here is the very stuff of fun in Taylor's time; incidentally it is in the manner of Nicholas Breton. Not only Breton but other writers of 'characters', such as Sir Thomas Overbury and John Stephens, use the same method with more subtlety. They pick a type of person and take an essential characteristic and then develop its implications with some exaggeration.

Taylor speaks of the Fishmongers and their prey:

> In the rearward comes Captain Crab, Lieutenant Lobster (whose catching claws always put me in mind of a sergeant), the blushing Prawn, the well-armed Oyster, the Scallop, the Welk, the Mussel, Cockle and the Periwinkle, these are hot shots, venereal provocators, fishy in substance and fleshly in operation.

Taylor is using the incongruous, humanizing fishes.

In all these passages one can detect the ecstatic pleasure in piling up words and in bringing to bear far-fetched figures of speech. In such language Shakespeare makes Petruchio address the tailor; Fluellen's speeches in *Henry V* are of the same kind. It was a common type of humour at that time, I suspect, both in Chiltern alehouses and London taverns, the expression of an expansive mood of high spirits. A little later, in the reign of Charles II, Roger Lowe, when he wished to tell two funny stories of his embarrassing experiences, fell into the same sort of language.

Taylor uses another kind of humour. He relates how he, a poor mechanical waterman, happened by chance to be riding in a coach with Sir William Waade, and suddenly felt overcome with importance:

> Such a tympany of pride puffed me up that I was ready to burst with the wind-colic of vain glory. In what state I would lean over the boot and look and pry if I saw any of my acquaintance, and then I would stand up, vailing my bonnet, kissing my right claw, extending my arms . . . with God save your Lordship, Worship, or How doest thou, honest neighbour, or good fellow?

Taylor was making fun of himself, of a humble man behaving like a great man, and he was perhaps poking a little fun at the way the great exhibited themselves to the public.

He makes fun of himself another time. He was cataloguing the towns near London and saying a little something about them. He mentions Queenborough in Kent and adds: 'This town is famous for my arrival there . . . with a boat of brown paper.' In one of his publicized expeditions Taylor had gone in a paper boat to Queenborough.

In one of his addresses to the Roundheads he comes close to dry humour:

> You have fought for our liberties and have taken them away from us: you have fought for the Gospel and you have spoiled the Church: you have fought for our goods and you have 'em.

Taylor must be granted something more. He was, I think, the first writer of nonsense verse. In *The Essence, Quintescence, Incence, Innocence, Lye-sence, and Magnificence of Nonsence upon Sence* (1653) he gives us nonsense verse and not without skill. Whether that nonsense had any influence on later nonsense-verse writing I am not prepared to say.

What a scribbler he was! What a capacity he had to say in many words what could have been said in few or left unsaid! Of that weakness he was not unaware. Before he introduced the great Eater of Kent he promised the reader the utter truth: 'I will not lie, on purpose to make all those liars that esteem me so.' Then he went on:

> Yet by your leave, Master Critic, you must give me license to flourish my phrases, to embellish my lines, to adorn my oratory, to embroider my speeches, to interlace my words, to draw out my sayings, and to bombast the whole suite of the business for the time of your wearing.

Precisely. He bombasted the whole business.

The reader has been able to realize from the extracts here quoted how unrhythmical was his verse, how diluted and commonplace his thought. What a mass of unnecessary allusions he made to classical writers! Sometimes he worked over the ideas of others (as those of Shakespeare, of Nash and of Nicholas Breton) and when he did so, invariably made them worse. He used puns constantly, as did the common people of his time. There was his 'watchful cloak' which had had no nap for seven years and he never grew weary of talking of the 'Amsterdamnable heretics'. He liked to say that when he went into a certain house he was wet to the skin and that when he left he was as dry as he had ever been in his life. He published a series of epigrams, as he called them, neither terse, nor pointed.

What was it that induced people to read his spate of doggerel? It may be suspected that he capitalized on his friendliness and natural high spirits. Around every corner he could meet acquaintances and he could readily persuade them to subscribe to his reports on his travels. He was a good fellow and deserved a good turn. Travel books about England were rather a new thing and might be entertaining. Furthermore the people of the time liked rhymes; they still repeated Thomas Tusser's couplets about farming practice and they had in their heads all sorts of local rhymes about peaks and downs and famous families. It is probably true that Taylor knew what people wanted. His aim was to

> make myself admired immediately
> Of such as understand no more than I.

He put the everyday thoughts of common people into language that was simple and yet seemed to have a touch of learning about it.

> Yet I at learning have a kind of aim.

He knew what he was about.

We can forgive Taylor for his mass of bad verse because he knew the worst about himself. He called himself one

> Who with good poets dare compare no way.

He was even more definite:

> I do want wit t'invent, conceive, and write
> To move myself or others to delight.

OLIVER HEYWOOD

OLIVER HEYWOOD

OLIVER HEYWOOD left so many notes about his daily life and activities that, when they were published nearly two centuries after his death, they added up to four thick volumes of small print. Those octavos have been seldom examined either by the public or even by inquiring scholars. To readers in our day they would seem revelations of Puritanism in its most zealous and ridiculous aspects. Yet they repay study by minds willing to put themselves back into the time and milieu of the writer and to allow themselves some sympathy for him and his kind. Such people were not unimportant in history. Heywood and other Nonconformist ministers of his half-century were the precursors of Methodism. It was generations of such devoted men who left to England the legacy of the Nonconformist Conscience. From Heywood's jottings we learn about an evangelistic minister and the serious-minded hearers who filled his chapel and other chapels. We learn also about the less worthy but no less typical North-country men of the time, rough, hard-fisted people with plans in their heads. They were not the Englishmen we think of at once, but they were of a kind not to be overlooked or forgotten; they and their like were to bring about the Second Industrial Revolution and make Britain the first great manufacturing nation. In doing so they transformed cloth-making villages and towns into centres of mechanized industry; they spread out and turned a landscape of terraced moors and remote dales into the Black Country of furnaces and factories and long, drab streets. An up-and-coming stock they had been of old but also somewhat undisciplined and often lawless, and the earnest evangelist was frequently horrified at their conduct but hoped nevertheless to turn them into obedient followers of his God.

He was the right man for the place and people and time, a born exhorter of sinners. From childhood he had been marked out, as he liked to believe, for the ministry. As a boy he would preach to his playmates, a practice which inclined his parents to dedicate him to the service of the Lord. When an old woman, observing his strong voice, had asked him if he would be a preacher, he had replied: 'Yes, if I might be a good one.'

The education he received proved not unsuitable for his future calling. Sent from one school to another he happened at last upon a teacher who taught him more in one year than he had learned from others in four. His teacher he regarded as of little worth, by which he may have meant that his master did not emphasize religion, but he was grateful for the 'good humane' literature he had been led to read and hoped that he had sucked the juice from the ancient writers without the woeful contagion.

He entered Cambridge University in 1647 when Puritans were dominant in the University. There he gathered much of divine knowledge from his tutor, Mr. Hammond, who preached at Giles Church, and from 'ingenious and gracious scholars'. The secular learning he received from the ancient writers he respected, provided that it did not degenerate into 'witty inventions' and 'idle aesthetical discourses'. Later in his life he came to believe that if he had given up more time to the classical authors he might have proved more useful in his profession. But already his mind was set on practical divinity and experimental truth, which he regarded as more vital to his soul. By experimental truth he meant, I think, the insight gained from experience in prayer.

When he was about twenty he came down from Trinity College with five years to wait before, under Presbyterian rules, he could be ordained as a minister. He hoped to find some well-known divine in whose home he could live and be further trained. But after six months at home he became 'entangled in a preaching work'. After a few trials as a preacher in out-of-the-way places he began presently to appear more publicly. His uncle, Francis Critchlaw, suggested his name to the members of Coley Chapel in the parish of Halifax. Heywood preached before them and the hearers were so impressed that they asked this youth of twenty-one to be their minister.

Coley Chapel was one of twelve chapelries connected with Halifax parish. It was to the north-west of Halifax in the hamlet of Northowram, a half-mile from Coley on the Halifax–Bradford road. The country was full of substantial houses inhabited by families who had done well in business, mostly in the clothing business, and of the cottages of clothing and mining workers.

The country was described by Defoe, who came from Lancashire through that part of the West Riding, as Heywood had done many times before, over the awesome pass of Blackstone Edge. Defoe had been impressed with the number of people, with the quality of the inns and with the extent of the cloth and mining industries, and hardly less with the height of the hills and the deep snow upon them in winter. In each valley Defoe entered, the houses seemed closer together than in the valley he had passed through. Every three or four acres had a house attached to it. As he approached Halifax the country seemed one continuous village. At almost every house there was a tenter, and on almost every tenter a piece of cloth, or a kersey, or a shalloon. He had marked the sun gleaming on thousands of white cloths.

What gratified Defoe most was the busyness of everyone; not a beggar was to be seen, except in an occasional alehouse. The people were enterprising, concerned to make a living, many of them Nonconformists.

Among such people Heywood had grown up and he had much to give them. It would be wrong to say that religion was the outstanding part of his life, it was more than that. All that he thought or said or did was involved with his faith. He was continually seeking God because he was continually losing him. The intensity of his spiritual life did not make for serenity but it did in some degree explain his power over his audiences.

A man of his intensity should have had a violent conversion. It troubled Heywood that as a young man he had had no such experience. He believed that before he was twelve years of age God had touched his heart but not in the striking manner to be expected. He had had many shakings and convulsions of the heart. He would walk in the field and be ready to roar out the bitterness of his soul. Finally he was convinced by the experience of others and by the 'conclusion of Mr. Baxter' that the Holy Spirit might work in quiet ways.

His own worthlessness and the majesty of God troubled him:

> Oh my Lord, I am here at Thy footstool, a worthless worm, an unprofitable branch, a sinful wretch, fit for nothing but to be cast out as unsavory salt.

Again and again he referred to himself as a poor worthless worm: He seemed to find a sense of exaltation in self-abasement:

> So that people may do that which is honest I matter not if I be counted as a castaway . . . Let the King live, though I die; let Christ reign as King though I serve as a slave.

To those given to such moods of exaltation there came naturally hours of reaction when their souls did not respond to prayer and meditation. Then what mental flagellation they endured: they had sinned, and they searched their memories for the cause, in many cases successfully. But they were always certain that it was their fault that they could not rise to spiritual ecstasy.

It was worse for Heywood as a preacher. It behoved him at all times to be on the crest of the wave, to be constantly filled with assurance of support from his God. When he was preaching he would kindle to the subject and would gather, as he believed, new strength from his source of strength. Scores of times when he mentioned in his diary his preaching he would add: 'God helped.' At other times he would come away from the delivery of a sermon with a sense of failure.

Such a preacher called forth emotion in his hearers, as he intended. There was developing in the North a religion marked by excitement. Groans, ejaculations and especially tears came to be regarded as the outward proof that the heart had been touched. In the autumn of 1679 Heywood noted:

> I preached at John Heys to a full assembly. God wonderfully helped in prayer; such tears, groans, that sometimes my voice was scarce heard for the noise of the people's cries. I have seldom heard the like – a good sign.

His records have many descriptions of such scenes.

> God did wonderfully help my heart and many others, so that I saw many tears dropped from many eyes.

Of one occasion when he was praying for a woman in childbirth he wrote:

> Oh how sweetly did God carry out my heart in many passionate groans and tears.

The fervency of the North-country Nonconformists must have been exhausting. Fast days in particular were hard on them. When they abstained from food they did mount, as they believed, to spiritual heights, but could not escape the reaction. On one occasion after such a fast Heywood observed that his heart was warmed but that his body was disordered and next morning he complained of a violent headache. Many such headaches he had, and it is easy to suspect that they were not unrelated to his spiritual ordeals. He was tempted

> to abate and remit of my zeal and fervency in devotion, and to be more moderate, as I see others are; and that word comes in oft: I will have mercy and not sacrifice. But when I consider of the saints weeping, pouring out their souls like water before the Lord, crying mightily effectual fervent prayers . . . I dare not do otherwise, if God help, whatever becomes of this poor carcass.

Heywood could have pointed out many passages in Scripture, and especially in the Old Testament, to support this faith in the efficacy of emotion openly expressed. No doubt he must also have discovered for himself that when he uttered his most passionate appeals to sinners he was most likely to convert them. In his zeal for their salvation he went further. He had a way of marking down passages that would 'pierce and wound' his hearers, that is, I suppose, touch upon the particular weaknesses of an individual and bring home to him a sense of guilt.

Was he then a 'hell-fire preacher', the reader may ask. I think not. In those discourses of his which have been printed he says less than one would expect about the wrath to come, though he does mention the 'sulphurous lake' and alludes to children crying amidst infernal torments because their parents had failed to give them religious instruction. In general one would gather from his sermons that he stressed the goodness of God more than His wrath.

Five volumes of his theological writings had been published (1842) nearly half a century before his diaries appeared, most of them his longer discourses, which he had either printed in his lifetime, or prepared for printing, and a few of them sermons. They were not passionate appeals to sinners but moderate discussions of the Christian life as conceived by a Puritan, set forth in a tone of sweet reasonableness. The author was more learned than one would suppose from his own account of himself. In his memoranda he tells us of his inability to conceive of abstruse pieces of learning or of knotty controversies and describes his embarrassment in the presence of those who made nice distinctions. When he brought out his *Family Altar* he indicated that another minister had published a better book, 'sinewy', and more 'suitable to the learned', but that his book was more adapted to the common use of country people. He did not indulge in subtleties nor pursue logic far but wrote simply and clearly and carried his reader with him. He had searched the Scriptures and he understood the Greek of the New Testament and the Hebrew of the Old Testament and could examine Greek and Hebrew words for their original meanings. Moreover he was versed in the Church Fathers and familiar with Calvin and Luther. The Puritan theologians from Perkins down to Baxter he could quote. What is more interesting is that he cited those good Anglicans, Joseph Hall and Richard Hooker, and used again and again the works of the 'divine Herbert', i.e. George Herbert. The study of books he enjoyed; by them he had 'good opportunity to lay in', as he had 'many to lay out'.

How those formal discourses he published compared with the sermons he delivered on ordinary occasions we would like to know. Something we learn from his diaries of the way in which he prepared sermons. He would take up his Bible and leaf over the pages, hoping to come upon an appropriate text and subject. If he failed to do so, or if the outline he had drawn up disappointed him, he would fall on his knees and seek guidance from above and would record happily: 'I was helped in my study.' Occasionally he was forced by circumstances to deliver extempore sermons, and, as he thought, with good success. No doubt in such sermons he drew largely upon his general learning and his sense of the situation. He would look over his audience as individuals and think of their shortcomings and of their needs.

His success in preaching would have turned the head of many

a man. When Heywood found himself pleased at the good opinion his sermons elicited from others he would reproach himself for vanity. One Sabbath morning in 1670 after a sermon he wrote sorrowfully:

> Found much assistance – yet was conscious of guilt before I came out of the pulpit – such hearts we have!

Sometimes the sin of pleasure in success seemed graver to him. When he saw his friend Priestley take down Dr. Dawson's sermon and not his own, he discovered within himself workings of pride and envy. When he visited friends in Leeds he could not but notice that he was not urged to preach before them.

Such experiences were unusual. In most instances he was implored to preach. When he came to Holdsworth, 'the town seeing me come flocked a great company thither'. However much he struggled to keep down his pride in the following he had gained, he could not but be happy that the servants of the Lord were listened to.

But it cut him to the quick that he was mocked by the less godly. An Oxford scholar drinking with his friends had made fun of Heywood's manner of speaking: 'He canted, as he pretended, like me . . . Very profane, sitting in the chair of the scornful . . . Father forgive them.' To ridicule a spokesman of God was indeed a sin that needed forgiveness and Heywood would be the one to ask it. We can understand the young man from Oxford. Heywood's language abounded in imagery, not all of it seemly.[1]

His prayers were even more effective than his sermons. They were intimate, almost conversational, communings with the Almighty, who seemed to him to be in the room with him. Much of his time at home he was on his knees. He would have a

[1] 'All the voracious fowls of the air cannot catch one least chicken from our dear Lord, that is hatched by the saving influence of God's spirit.' IV, 45.

'melting session' and feel his Master close to him and then he would be less fortunate and feel that the face of the Lord was turned from him. We have seen that in his public performances he often believed that his sermon had not been a success, but that when he had come to pray things had gone better. Sometimes both sermon and prayer went well. At his sister's house: 'I preached and prayed four hours. Oh what a frame was my heart in.' His prayers seemed to hypnotize his hearers; they could not escape the feeeling that the Lord was indeed there in the room with them.

So much faith did these North-country people come to have in his prayers that he was constantly being summoned to come at once and pray with those seriously ill. He was implored also to intercede for those at a distance whom he could not visit in person. Such people, when he sought the Lord for their recovery, usually took an almost immediate turn for the better, occasionally at the very moment when he had been on his knees in their behalf. It is not surprising that he was asked to use his influence with his God for other purposes. In times of drought he prayed for rain and in seasons of wet weather for sunshine, and he could not but observe how quickly his prayers were answered.

Surprisingly enough the religion of this man of feeling was, at least in his later years, saner than one would expect. He accepted the tenets of the Presbyterians but interpreted them broadly. All men, he believed, ought to be pressing towards the same goal, although they might be going along different paths. Two 'conformable ministers', that is, ministers who had accepted the Established Church, he characterized as 'choice holy men'. He welcomed the union of the Presbyterians and the Congregationalists, and did what he could to promote it. The doctrines and power of the Papacy he feared profoundly and there was much in the Church of England that gave him pause. But he cherished the policy of tolerance. Among his memoranda is this statement:

> When I begun first in my profession of Christianity . . . my charity was far narrower and my forbearance shorter than I see it must be, upon further experience; for if I judge all obstinate that have sinned foully, and all unregenerate that cannot evidence it to me, I may offend God and wrong them.

Among his rules of practice he laid down:

> Be catholic both in principles and practices: neither confine thy love to a party, nor thy obedience to one or more duties. Partiality is a note of hypocrisy; universality of sincerity.

His calling included pastoral work. He officiated at baptisms, marriages and funerals. He visited the sick, prayed with women before and after their ordeals in childbearing, and comforted those in distress. A woman whose son had been hanged at Cambridge came to him 'weeping for her son', and he went off next day to pray with her and her husband. Again and again he was asked for advice about personal matters, such as marriage and family problems, advice he found it hard to give. Nevertheless we find him following a man into a field to rebuke him for shortcomings. Yet he was not as ready as many of his persuasion to be his brother's keeper.

The relation of the Nonconformist minister to his flock was unlike that of the Anglican clergyman to his parishioners. The minister preached from the Scriptures which were almost as familiar to his listeners as to him. No learned language intervened between pulpit and pew. The minister had not been imposed upon the people from above nor was he of another world from them. They themselves had selected him because of his ability to expound the Word and because his character seemed to them to lend force to his exposition.

These Nonconformists among whom Heywood lived in the district of Craven in the North Riding of Yorkshire were a special breed of people, even in the North country. They were enterprising business folk, as we have seen. 'They excel the rest', wrote an Elizabethan squire, 'in policy and industry.' They had, he declared, a 'natural ardency in new inventions . . . in their faculty of cloth'. If the rest of the country would follow them, he believed, the wealth of Yorkshire would be doubled.

Their skill in business was not their most extraordinary characteristic. They were a rough, almost wild people with rude and arrogant manners. That they still beheaded thieves, said the Elizabethan squire, was because they needed to do so. An early nineteenth-century writer who knew the country intimately noted the tone of defiance in every voice and the air of fierceness in every countenance. He believed manners and morals to be more degraded there than in any other part of the island. Old families, he explained, 'the great correctors of barbarism', had long been extinct. T. D. Whitaker may have overstated matters but we shall see from Heywood's own stories that in the late seventeenth century these talented people were not wholly amenable to the law or to the customs of polite society.

Paradoxically enough, they were men who since the Reformation had been very religious, with a strong leaning towards Puritanism. The best of them were good people who worked hard, paid their debts – not too common a virtue in seventeenth-century England – and tried to serve their God. The worst of them were not God-fearing, in the ordinary sense of that word, but were nevertheless afraid of the God of the Old Testament and hoped, however much they had offended Him, to make peace with Him in the end and avoid the terrors of hell. Meanwhile such people made a hell on this earth for themselves and for others.

With the strength and weakness of these people Heywood was

thoroughly familiar. He did not expect deference from them. He demanded deference only to the Almighty, and even the worst of them had traces of that. Such rough customers once converted made serious and earnest Christians, even if they did not always display loving-kindness to one another.

Quarrelsomeness over property was the besetting sin even of the best of them. They fell out over lands and bargains. Those engaged in a long quarrel with their brethren would realize that they must not take part in the Lord's Supper, since they had not forgiven their enemies, and Heywood would note their absence and visit them. It was a grief to him to think how the ungodly would gloat over the differences of the godly and he would do his best to bring the quarrelling parties together, praying with them and about them, and urging them to shake hands and make up. Sometimes he persuaded them to accept arbitration, sometimes he could do nothing with them and gained only resentment for his interference.

With the Restoration (1660) Heywood and his Presbyterian friends, who had supported the return of Charles II and had expected toleration, found themselves within two years the target of repressive legislation. By the Act of Uniformity passed in 1662 those ministers who would not use the service of the Prayer Book and assent in full to it, and who would not be reordained episcopally if they had not been so ordained, found themselves marked for ejection from their ministerial posts. On August 24th, 1662, 'Black Bartholomew's Day', two thousand ministers, more or less, had to give up their positions and their incomes. Heywood was of course forced out of his post at Coley Chapel. Moreover, he was excommunicated, so that he was forbidden to attend any church service anywhere and in addition fined for non-attendance. The Act of Uniformity struck at Nonconformist ministers. The Conventicle Act of 1664 put heavy penalties upon those who attended any religious services except those of the Church of England. Any group of five or more people, above the members of a household, who gathered to worship constituted a 'conventicle', and those in attendance could be heavily fined and for the third offence transported. But an even harsher act followed – the Five-Mile Statute of 1666 – by which Nonconformist ministers were forbidden to come within five miles of any parish, town or place in which they had served as ministers. The Nonconformist preachers had to leave their homes and move elsewhere.

As a result of the various Acts of Parliament which came to be known as the Clarendon Code, the Nonconformists were estopped from all services. What were they to do? Many of them held responsible positions in their communities and could ill afford to ignore the law of the land. Some of them accepted the situation and attended the Anglican services, a few of the ministers became 'conformable' and were granted posts. But the majority of Nonconformist laymen and ministers awaited better days and meanwhile carried on their assemblies in secret. They had never taken the law too seriously. Heywood himself hesitated at first. He was loyal to the King and proud to think that he had been opposed to the usurper, Cromwell. But he was above all things a preacher. Should he obey the law of man and deny his Master? When he was invited to discourse in private houses he could not say no. Presently he was preaching all over the moor country.

The more the Nonconformists were legislated against the more their ministers smuggled their services to the people. The worshippers appear briefly in Heywood's pages, slipping in the early dawn or after nightfall across the fields to an isolated cottage or barn. Usually they had a sentinel posted near by to inform them of the approach of bailiffs or constables and had hiding-places arranged for the preacher and sometimes for the audience. Seldom were there more than forty or fifty Nonconformists together at a service, but now and then more turned up. Once indeed 500 people gathered at five in the morning as a result of a brief notice sent round the evening before. It is surprising how rarely they were disturbed by the constables. It must be that those officials often closed their eyes to the strange traffic directed to out-of-the-way places. The truth is that the local authorities hesitated in many instances to deal drastically with the lawbreakers. Not a few justices of the peace were on their side and neglected their duties as officials. Many of the lawbreakers were useful men in business and worthy of respect as citizens; a few of them were members of well-known gentle families who allowed the forbidden services to be held in their houses.

Heywood recorded some of his experiences. On a wintry night of the day after Christmas he met a group at Elias Hinchball's at Bramley. Heywood had finished preaching and the group gathered together was sitting about the fire smoking when the constable and the churchwardens arrived and demanded who were present and what they were doing. The Nonconformists sat still and offered the specious excuse that 'friends may visit one another this Christmas time'. The churchwardens knew well enough that the Nonconformists did not observe Christmas and took the names of all present. 'What they intend to do, the Lord only knows,' wrote Heywood, 'but we had done our work.' A young tailor in return for a fee had played the informer against them.

Many times Heywood had to cut short his preaching and prayers; he had to be smuggled out of a back door into a barn. In such operations there was some want of dignity, but the Nonconformists were not greatly concerned with dignity. They were so intent indeed upon the service of God that they were not always scrupulous. The bailiff of Halifax told Heywood that he would have to summon him to the Quarter Sessions.

OLIVER HEYWOOD

> My friends went to this Jepson, gave him good words, a small pittance of money from me. He promised he would not go to the Sessions.

On another occasion Heywood wrote:

> God brought off the constable of our town, James Scolfield, very well, he informed upon oath that though he came upon the most likely place for a conventicle—yet he saw no people but the family (that was my house) – so he came off well; they did accept of his bill.

It would appear that the constable who was under oath took pains not to enter the house and so discover what was going on. Heywood was gratified that the man had practically perjured himself in their behalf. Later we find out that James Scolfield was himself one of the Nonconformist group to which Heywood ministered. More than once Heywood observed that when the bailiffs set out to break his assembly the Lord directed them another way. Heywood was asking a good deal of his Lord to make men fail in their duty.

Twice Heywood suffered heavily. In July 1670 he was fined £10 and could not pay. The officers came with a warrant upon his possessions and took away three good chests, three tables, chairs, stools and bedding, and so on. Heywood made capital out of his misfortune, preaching that afternoon on the text: 'For ye had compassion on me in my bonds, and took joyfully the spoiling of your goods, knowing in yourselves that you have a better and more enduring substance' (Heb. x, 34). In June of the following year his goods were again seized, this time without warrant. From January 1685 until the following December he was imprisoned in York Castle. It was a distressingly idle interlude in his life, but he suffered little harm. The jailor consulted his convenience, obtaining a private room for him by turning out a Conformist clergyman. 'Many precious servants of God out of the city' came to visit him, his wife was allowed to be with him part of the time, and he had opportunity to study and to write, as if in his own house.

His arrests and imprisonments Heywood endured with what grace he could. It was the continuous suspense that was hardest to bear. He never knew when he was likely to be arrested and carried off to jail. The humiliation of being a hunted man wore down his spirit. He once summed up his troubles:

> Twice have I been excommunicated, thrice imprisoned, once plundered, banished from my own house, often sought for by warrants, many times made to flee . . . been threatened, watched, often vexed with disputes, . . . railings, grievous contempt and scorn from those that are at ease.

The last phrase is significant. He was seldom at his ease. The business of worshipping in stealth and living in fear continued from 1662 to 1687 with one blessed interval.[1] In 1672 temporary licences were given to Nonconformists to preach and Heywood was one of the first to receive such a licence. Even during that time the episcopal powers in York did what they could to make it hard for him. In 1675 the licences were revoked and Heywood found himself again in constant danger.

His tribulations he never regretted. He came out of York jail with increased pride in 'this great work of soul-catching'. When men and women from afar off sought him out to tell him of a sermon delivered by him years before which had set them on the right road, he was gratified. When townsmen who had been arrayed on the Anglican side petitioned that he might preach in

[1] In April 1687 James II issued his Declaration of Indulgence. Heywood, unlike many Nonconformists who anticipated the growth of popery, approved. 'Oh what a change!' he wrote. 'Surely somebody hath laid hard siege at the throne of grace.' But he and his brethren were not really secure until parliamentary, as well as royal, indulgence was granted by the Toleration Act (1689).

Coley Chapel, he wrote: 'This is strange . . . that they should thus own a poor despised, persecuted minister, that's cast out as a vessel wherein is no pleasure'. When two young men testified in prayer, 'with many savoury expressions', what Heywood had done for their souls, the old evangelist was touched. Such accomplishments were just what he had been pleading for to God. He wished to leave it on record that were he to choose his calling he would choose this calling above that of the richest merchant in the Royal Exchange, or the greatest monarch on his throne. He was probably more sincere than most who indulge in such statements.

The Clarendon Code had forced Heywood to travel, to become an itinerant evangelist. When the evil days came upon the Nonconformists they looked to him and and men like him for assurance. He was welcomed all over Yorkshire and the neighbouring counties and became a kind of vicar-general in those parts to the Dissenting brethren. A travelling salesman for the Gospel, he was kept busy.

Take one fortnight, for example. On Monday he set out for Little Horton where he stayed with the John Sharps and preached. On Tuesday he preached at Mr. Rawden's house at Rawden, on Wednesday at Josephy Kitchin's house at Farsley, where he had 'a good auditory'. On Thursday he was in Leeds, on Friday he moved south to Wakefield, and the next day he continued southward to Sir Edward Rhodes at Houghton and spent the Sunday there, 'with much comfort'. Monday and Tuesday he visited friends in Wath, spent Thursday at Swath Hall, home of the Wadsworth family. On Friday he lodged with the Nathaniel Bottomleys near by and preached there. On Saturday he went to Penistone and had a Sabbath there, precious to his soul, that of course included a sermon. For the next three days he worked back towards Halifax, visiting a sick woman, dining with a German major, missing his way over a moor in a mist, and taking refuge for two nights with a friend at Hopton Hall. He arrived home to find all well. His boys were reading the books assigned them, learning the catechisms, and able to recite from memory chapters of the Bible.

He was soon again on his travels. He has listed in his characteristically orderly fashion the number of weekday sermons he preached, the fasts, the days of thanksgiving he took part in. In the 1680s the weekday sermons were always over one hundred, that is an average of two a week. He put down also the mileage he covered. From 1685 to 1691 he travelled over a thousand miles per year. In 1681 and 1687 he covered fourteen hundred miles.

He was thus much of the time on horseback. Many moors he crossed, often in snowy weather on narrow, icy paths, along fearful edges. He was a heavy man and possibly somewhat awkward on a horse. Bad falls he experienced again and again but escaped serious injury. The horses he rode had to be trustworthy solid beasts. His favourite was Old Dick. For fifteen years he rode this horse. 'Oh, what sweet seasons hath my soul had many a time when riding on my old Dick.' Guy, a later acquisition, was not as sympathetic a companion: 'I begin a reflection or meditation on a moor or solitary lane, but follow it not to purpose as formerly.'

With all his travels Heywood liked things at home,

> the daily accommodations I have had, wholesome meat, handsome clothes, sweet sleep, fire to sit by, good chamber to sit in, books to read, pen and ink, my memory, invention, the use of my eyes, ears, hands, feet, all members in due order.

He was devoted to his house at Coley, where he had brought his first wife, 'where my heart is more than any place in the world besides'. It was situated among his neighbours. It was there that God had blessed his labours more than in any other place.

He liked his neighbours and indeed he liked people of many kinds. He kept something like open house. Every Sunday there were six or eight people at his board and bi-monthly when the sacrament was celebrated he might receive as many as twenty people for Sunday dinner besides others who were furnished 'broth and bread'. Visitors were always turning up on other days. 'I had too much company', he would write. Yet when he remained undisturbed all day he noted it with a kind of disappointment. He had friends all round the country and in every class. He knew a few peers of the realm and he stayed overnight with many Nonconformist gentry who opened their houses for his prayer-meetings and sermons and who protected him when a hunted man. In York he would stay with Lady Hewley or Lady Watson or Lady Hewet. So far as one can judge from his brief allusions to them in his diaries he treated the rich and great with the same consideration as the poor and hard-driven. He was unlike the canting Nonconformists in plays and novels who played up to their wellborn friends. No doubt he was most at home with the hard-working, cloth-making families.

That he could carry on with so much company means that his household machinery must have been smooth-running. His mind was kept free for other and to him more vital concerns. Heywood was twice married; the first time very happily, the second time successfully enough. His first wife, Elizabeth Angier, was the daughter of a well-known minister, John Angier. Reared in a family given over to spiritual activities, Elizabeth had developed her own religious life. It pleased her husband that she had acquired a great knowledge of the Bible and that she could repeat a sermon methodically. But she had a 'fearful nature', and Heywood had often to cheer her in moods of despondency about her faith. Moreover she disliked controversy, like many women, and believed above all in Christian charity.

In one thing only was Elizabeth Angier at fault: she loved Oliver Heywood too well. Heywood gave a brief narrative of how they came together: 'Her inclination towards me at the first view . . . my disappointments other ways . . . Her constancy to me, my gradual complacence in her.' His one criticism of her was the vehemence of her affection, a strange suggestion from an emotional man.

After the marriage (April 1655) Heywood and Elizabeth lived in the closest harmony for six years. She managed his household with skill and foresight. She was content with her husband's situation and asked nothing more of life. But the birth of three sons and four miscarriages proved too much for her.

> She finding weakness increasing the winter before she died (she) took much time to set house and heart in order for her great change, and did everything as one that was ready to take her flight . . . She would have no clothes bought except for present use . . . She provided linen for us that we might have nothing to buy of one year at least.

Heywood took her to Lancashire to her father's home, hoping that the change of air might do her good.

> As we went along she often bade farewell to Yorkshire and was persuaded she should never return that way again, as indeed it proved.

Physicians in Manchester were consulted but they could do nothing. She died about May of 1661. Heywood's words about her carry conviction:

> I want her at every turn, everywhere, and in every work. Methinks I am but half myself without her.

Heywood was left with two small sons, John and Eliezar (the third had died two years before). He kept one maid, Martha, a convert of his, devoted to him, who ran the household satisfactorily.

After six years Heywood began to consider a second marriage, a course the incomparable Elizabeth had recommended. He married Abigail Crompton (June 1667) of Breighmet, Lancashire, a spinster of thirty-two:

> I was married by Mr. Hide at Salford Chapel by Manchester in a decent manner: we were under twenty persons of the nearest relations, and I am abundantly satisfied in my gracious yoke-fellow.

Was there a defensive note in his words as if his relatives had not been quite satisfied? At that time a woman unmarried at thirty-two was hard to find. We may guess that her charms were not unusual. Again and again she appears in Heywood's notes simply as 'my wife'.

Abigail was, however, a kind and loving partner; she kept house well enough. But she had her differences with him about his friendliness to Martha Tetlaw who had been his servant for many years and was now married to a man in the neighbourhood. Abigail resented the calls he made on the Tetlaw family and accused Martha of gossip about her. His wife's jealousy elicited from him no signs of guilty conscience. It is a wonder that she was not more often jealous of him. He was always going to pray with women before their ordeals. 'I kept a fast with many women for Esther Kershaw's safe deliverance in childbearing.' He was always comforting women who had troubles of conscience or were semi-melancholic about their sins. It must be that he carried himself with prudence, for Abigail accepted such pastoral duties without complaint. Now and then she had words with him. On one occasion he dealt plainly with her lest malice lodge in her heart and Satan gain the advantage. In their quarrels he would draw her to her knees and engage in joint prayer at great length until they were reconciled, possibly when she recognized that he was in the right. For Heywood was likely to believe himself in the right. In his later years he was surrounded by men and women who offered him adoration for the spiritual guidance he had given them, and he may have come to think of himself as the spokesman of his Lord. A man devoted to the Lord's service can persuade himself that whatever thwarts him is a disservice to his Master. He may have been a trying husband, and she was certainly a helpful wife. She watched over him with care, indeed her efforts to prevent him from overdoing and to keep him at home when he was under the weather seemed to annoy him. But it is clear that Abigail by her great devotion to his God slowly made up for her other failings. More and more often he took her with him on his journeys over the country, and at home the two were constantly praying together. When she was ill he showed concern.

It has been pointed out that Heywood was a traveller through Yorkshire and Lancashire and even up to Westmorland and down into Nottinghamshire. On those journeys he had his eyes open to observe the men and women in the North country. Not all of them were God-fearing, as we have seen earlier. Many of them were restless, driving and even cruel folk, like their Viking ancestors. They were keen on the brass, to use a modern Yorkshire idiom. Prototypes of the later industrialists could be found all over the North. Heywood's own father, an active and earnest Nonconformist, had been 'always contriving something, repairing, transposing, or building'. He had made himself well-to-do and then had over-extended himself and lost his small fortune. The country was full of more successful business men. Jeremiah Bentley bought a wood for £10,000, built a stately malthouse, leased mills, and tore down old structures to develop new dwellings with shops below and apartments above. He died in middle age a rich man.

Yorkshiremen were thrifty. Heywood recorded many narratives of 'covetous', 'scraping', 'sparing' people. Susanna Appleyard had brought a great portion to her husband who was 'an exacting, provident man'; they had two sons and two daughters.

The older boy, John, was their favourite, 'helpful, forward for good things, yet very sparing, whom they doted on'. The younger, Samuel, though a charming boy, was 'prodigal, at least very generous'; he was disowned, ran off to fight in Scotland and died. When the father died, the economical John turned his mother out of the house; she 'wandered in the night, drazzled and amazed', until she came to the home of her daughter. There she was refused shelter and was finally given refuge by neighbours. Later her son, possibly compelled to do so by the parish, rented a poor room for her in Halifax where she lived until her death.

Heywood was shocked by the stories of sin and shame that came to his ear but lingered nevertheless almost lovingly over them, leaving out none of the macabre details. They gave him opportunity to moralize about the punishment of the wicked and reinforced his conviction of the need for evangelism. They reveal not only the morals of many of the less godly people of the moors but their hardness and their gloating interest in the misfortunes of others. They were the ancestors of the characters in the Brontë novels, but worse. A fine young gentlewoman was found in travail by the roadside by some young men. She had begotten a malformed stillborn infant. As she lay groaning she denied her name, although recognized, and insisted that she was a certain man's wife. 'All the neighbourhood came flocking about her', to her bitter dismay. 'They got her into our meeting house', and sent for her sisters and brothers, who 'made such exclamations of the shame' and conveyed her away to Halifax. The pitiable creature wished she were out of the world. But even more to be pitied was a pregnant woman without means of support. The constable and the churchwardens were likely to push her out of the parish so that the community would not have to support her and her child. Heywood tells of a poor woman driven out in the snow to bear her child. The babe was frozen to death and the mother 'distracted'. We learn of a female servant washing clothes who was delivered of a child which she casually buried and returned to her washing. She had been observed and was finally executed. Heywood himself watched barbarous scenes. A woman either drunk or mad was being hurried on a sledge to the house of correction and was being fearfully whipped, followed by a shouting mob. She was thrown at length on a dunghill and left there for the night. Heywood remarked: 'Oh horrid cruelty.' Often he would conclude an episode with the exclamation: 'Oh fearful', or 'Oh for a judgment'. He recorded many stories of happenings at cock-fights, at horse-races and tavern meetings where ale and brandy led to high words and casualties. He was at his best in tracing the unhappy progress of downward careers. He wrote at great length of a woman who had inherited land and had taken on three husbands in succession. 'She was notoriously addicted to wantonness; she was a swinish drunkard and took delight to see others drunk.' We may omit the account of her death which Heywood elaborated; his description of her inflated corpse oozing drink and blood is not easily forgotten. Heywood had a pleasanter story, at least pleasanter to our ears. A man had been so startled by one of Heywood's sermons into a realization of his evil life that he could not sleep of nights. He set out to consult a godly Christian but halted at an alehouse and became so relaxed that he was able to sleep and was no longer interested in being converted. 'Oh dreadful state!' commented Heywood.

He had other tales. A bad baronet, Sir Frances Wortley, lived at Penistone, where Heywood often preached. Wortley's misdeeds were shocking but his great-grandfather's had been worse. He had quarrelled with the freeholders in his town, had managed to drive them out, and had taken down the buildings in which they lived to make a waste for deer, 'taking great delight to hear the deer bell'. But, wrote Heywood, 'it came to pass that before he died he belled like a deer and was distracted'.

That yarn is to be found elsewhere in the literature of the time and was no doubt part of the folklore which Heywood gathered. He was one of that great fraternity of myth-collectors, interested in untimely fates. A few of his narratives have a ballad quality about them.

He had an interest in sudden deaths, as if himself afraid of such an eventuality. What really worried him, I suppose, was that men dying suddenly did not have time to make their peace with God. He filled pages with registers of deaths. 'Mary Bentley of Moorfield 'ate her supper, took her pipe . . . gave a groan, died.' 'Nathaniel Webster . . . fell a raving, died before ten a clock, but would not hear of death, but said immediately before, "I shall be with the lads", (i.e. his workmen, being a dyer).' Many of the deaths he recorded were from childbirth, others were the outcome of accidents in the house, in the fields and in rivers. Floods were always a threat in the narrow dales between the sharp slopes of the moors. Great walls of water would come down from the hills after a rain and overwhelm those crossing at fords. 'September 11, 1673 there was the greatest flood that was ever known . . . and betwixt them a woman was seen to go down, having red waistcoat and blue coat, sometimes up, sometimes down in the water.'

However terrible were the deaths Heywood recorded, the funerals that followed were not unpleasant gatherings of friends. The means for festivity were seldom wanting and men came away from such assemblies in high spirits. Heywood himself held off from strong liquor but he was critical of those who supplied scanty refreshment on such occasions. He noted also the case of a 'covetous, scraping man', an old hearer of the Word, who on his death-bed said no word about his soul but took pains to have provided plenty of cakes for the funeral. Such Yorkshire realism Heywood could understand.

Melancholy seems to have been a common illness in the Pennines. These people, some of them, were given to moodiness.

They worried about their souls, lest they were not in a state of grace, or lest they had committed the unpardonable sin, and were thus driven sometimes to the borders of insanity. To such people Heywood made many visits but his prayers for them seem to have been less successful than for those with physical ailments. Occasionally the unhappy man, or more often woman, committed suicide. Hannah Worrall tried to find peace with the Anabaptists and then with the Quakers. She managed at length to hang herself. Since the rope she used proved too long to hold her body off the ground she bent her knees up.

Heywood was often downcast about the decline of faith. The schoolmaster of Hipperholm taught his scholars to beware of Nonconformity and made fun of it. Heywood had heard of Anglicans who declared their preference for Papacy over Presbyterianism and Heywood remarked grimly: 'It may be God will put them to it.' Like many he feared that the Catholics might gain control of the Government. It distressed him to see the Sabbath day misused. People spent their Sundays staying at home or loitering, or walking out to view cattle; they visited neighbours; they tarried in the alehouse. Even good people of whom Heywood otherwise thought well allowed themselves the pleasures of secular books and of histories on the holy day. In some places he observed that there were no sermons on the Sabbath afternoon.

There were other signs of irreligion. Some of the young men in his district went away to the universities and reported that the colleges in them were honeycombed with godlessness. It was said that the fellows never prayed with their scholars and that only common prayers (this was in 1679) were used. The tutor of a young man whom Heywood knew was believed to be an atheist or 'Hobbist'; he had no Bible in his room. Hobbes's *Leviathan* was thought to be his Bible.

Yet Heywood did not always go along with the extreme Nonconformists. He assumed the truth of witchcraft but when he ran into particular cases he had his doubts. He was called into pray over a young man strangely taken or 'possessed' and was inclined to believe that the young man was feigning. In another instance his doubts were considerable. A physician had declared the illness of a boy unnatural and had recommended that a cake made up of various ingredients, including some of the boy's hair and his urine, should be burned. At such a burning it was an old opinion that the witch who had caused the boy's illness would appear. The mother of the boy came to Heywood and to another Nonconformist minister to ask their judgment. The two ministers considered the matter and told her that the method prescribed had no foundation in nature or in Divine revelation. Heywood suggested prayer and fasting as cure for the illness.

He had an aversion to recreations and to the pleasures of this world. There was not time for them. One should give one's hours to one's calling and to the service of God, preparing for the next world. Heywood's mind was almost wholly on that world. In Manchester he had witnessed people rising at midnight to make garlands and strew flowers, 'bringing in the May', and had been the more annoyed because he had missed his sleep. Merriment of any kind seemed to distress him. John Mitchell kept open house the last week in the Christmas season and entertained all comers. Healths had been drunk and there had been 'fearful ranting work . . . Lord put a stop'. Cockfighting offended him. The ceremony of bearing rushes into the church seemed evil. In place of such worldly amusement the Nonconformists offered their brethren fasts, prayers and meditation. They did indeed make an effort to win young people to their way of life, but with purely religious inducements. The fortnightly 'young men's conference' which Heywood carried on in his house might be compared to the meetings of the Christian Endeavour societies of our time. Heywood made no compromise whatever with this world.

It comes as a surprise to learn that Heywood had some feeling for the beautiful. Once while riding over a high hill near Farnley he marked the lovely prospect all over the country, the sun shining gloriously. Fresh roses blooming at Christmas pleased him. Of course he was careful to draw a religious lesson from such sights. His God was a jealous one who tolerated few lapses from the consideration of His glory. Yet Heywood allowed himself to enjoy the 'sweet, pleasant, and melodious singing of birds about the house as delightfully as ever I heard in all my life, and I was much taken with the music'. But he hastened to add that the singing of the birds helped to cover up the sound of a forbidden meeting, and that as soon as the people left the meetings the birds were silent. The co-operation of the feathered creatures with the Nonconformists was no doubt the work of God.

Heywood had been concerned, as we have seen, about the evil course of young men. His own sons, as they grew up, were to give him worry. They had been brought up by their father – their mother had died when they were very young – to eschew all pleasures and to spend their time in memorizing chapters in the Bible and the catechisms and to give many hours to prayer. For his eldest boy, John, Heywood had great hopes:

> At night I set my two sons a praying: Eliezar begun and wept and prayed very feelingly, but John exceeded both in strong scriptural expostulations and sobbing and weeping [so] that sometimes he could hardly speak.

But such a routine may have proved tedious to growing boys who saw other lads enjoying themselves. As soon as they left home for school they changed their ways. Reports reached their father that John was drinking too much, disgracing himself and falling into debt. Whenever Heywood failed to hear from John he began to fear the worst. His anxiety, evident on almost every page of his notes, is painful to follow. As soon as the two boys came home the father would draw them into conference. John would work up great feeling over his failings and play the penitent with such abandon and with such expressions of regret as to convince his simple-minded parent that he was indeed a new person. But a relapse would follow. Sometimes the younger son was included in the disgrace and ultimate pardon. Meanwhile the father had to pay the debts the sons had incurred. In September 1676 the two boys returned from school with poor records but they accompanied their father into a private room and John showed virtuosity in prayer, 'groaning, weeping, pleading'. His father's heart was much melted and apparently satisfied.

The two sons were sent to Edinburgh University and the father worried about them there. Within a year they returned. Heywood seems to have drawn them both into helping him with preaching and to have been pleased and even moved by their sermons and prayers. For a while John seems to have taught. He was at length given a well-paid chaplaincy to a Nonconformist lady in London but lost that in disgrace. Eventually both sons justified in some degree the hopes of their father and became ministers. Heywood rejoiced to think that he had given two sons to the Lord but was not wholly at ease in his mind. Although the sons preached now and again to country congregations they preferred an easier life and accepted positions as chaplains in well-to-do families.

Heywood's finances tell us something of the man. His salary, which was about thirty pounds a year, seems to have been on a rather haphazard basis. Whenever he needed money he asked the members of his congregation for it and was gratified at their ready responses. He received extras, fees for weddings and probably for baptisms, and fees for sermons preached away from home. When he received no money for such sermons he recorded the fact in his diary. Altogether he did well, saved money and invested it in land. When he died he left property in Little Lever, Lancashire, and at Northowram, Sowerby and Ovenden in Yorkshire.

His modest competency made it possible for him to realize three dreams. In 1672 he bought himself the old house at Northowram to which he had brought his first wife. In 1688 he completed, with his own money and that of friends, a meeting house for his people, and in July of that year he preached his first sermon in the new structure. In 1693 he was able, by donating land, to set up a schoolhouse for poor scholars in his town. He used his savings for other ends. From 1684 on he contributed forty shillings a year to the poor and was able later to increase the gift.

Heywood had led an active life, riding, rain or shine, over rough moorland roads, and might have been fairly expected to show signs in early old age of what he had been through. But in his early sixties he gave little indication of slowing down. In his sixty-third year he had travelled almost a thousand miles, preached almost a hundred times, and kept nearly fifty fasts and fourteen days of thanksgiving. He had more invitations than in many years to occupy other pulpits, at Halifax, at Manchester and in London, invitations which pleased him but which he declined almost at once, preferring his own country church and his old parishioners.

> It's ill transporting a tree that thrives well in the soil . . . my poor gifts are more adapted to a meaner village than a great town.

Meanwhile he was turning out tracts on prayer and fasting. Those tracts added to his reputation among the Nonconformists. His London printer read over the manuscripts as they came in from Coley and pointed out statements which might be regarded as seditious. Heywood was usually willing to make the suggested excisions. He bought from his printer many copies of his discourses and distributed them among his friends.

The life of the time is dimly reflected in his notes. He had seen bishops up and down and up again. Here and there in his pages appear stories of men leaving for America, usually the poor and unsuccessful; some of them returned to England. He mentions the crowds shouting at the elections of knights of the shire. He distrusted the Catholic policy of James II and hailed the Glorious Revolution with gladness. In 1695 he was thanking God for William III and concerned at the plots against his life. He never ceased to fear that the Romanists might return. He noted something that was happening under the surface of history. A fellow-minister had spoken of the 'rot among the gentry'. Heywood reflected upon the gentle families in his own part of the country and observed that some were in prison, some in debt, some rooted out, title, name and all. 'Oh what unthriftness, wickedness, sloth, and God's curse for the same.' Heywood's explanations of social change were simple.

In old age he was inclined to go over his own life. Sinners had been saved and he had the reward of his travels. 'God will have the glory and I shall have the comfort.' He had suffered much for the 'good old cause of Puritanism and Nonconformity'. It warmed his heart to think he had been so far honoured as to bear God's name and wear his livery fifty-nine years. He had had more opportunities than fell to most:

> some good success and fruit of my poor labours, marry famous Mr. Angier's daughter, print so many books, enjoy so many comforts of life, bring up two sons to be ministers, build a chapel, help so many poor ministers and Christians in their necessities by myself and others, and yet have a competency for myself and wife to live upon.

It was more than he could have asked. His had been a happy pilgrimage and he knew well to whom the praise belonged, and yet there was that touch of personal satisfaction in his summary of accomplishments which even the godly seldom escape.

His whole life had been a struggle between his self-satisfaction over his service of his Lord and a fear of self-satisfaction. He was not unaware of the inferiority of some of the other Nonconformist preachers and of their jealousy of him. It was he, and he knew it, who could bring the chariots of Israel and the horsemen forward. Was it not God who had wonderfully advanced his credit among all sorts? He had good esteem among ministers and Christians and the affection of God's people. 'My dear Lord hath taken me into his wine-cellar.'

Yet at times he said to himself that he must beware of self-confidence and vainglory, and would humbly seek forgiveness of his Lord for those sins. He could not but notice that when he prayed the Lord did not always seem as close to him as in other days. No doubt his own capacity for emotion had been dulled by the years and thus he had a less vivid sense of his Master's presence.

He had to struggle not only with the sin of self-satisfaction but with that of envy. He thought of his adversaries:

> They enjoy their fat benefices, fair parsonages, and fruitful glebe; they step out of their houses into their churches, and read their easy services and say their eloquent orations, and eat the fat and drink the sweet, are companions of nobles and gentlemen.

It was hard not to yield to the sin of envy and the harder when he recalled all the perils he had been through and the opposition he had encountered from those very parsons. Yet even into his expression of envy there crept the note of self-satisfaction. His life and his troubles had been like those of the apostles.

He had been a vigorous and hardy man, troubled only with headaches, fits of ague and asthma. A brief trip to Knaresborough to take the waters there sufficed sometimes to bring about his recovery. Back in 1661 he had written that he desired to be dissolved and had set down seven reasons. Twelve years before his death he had prayed:

> O Lord . . . let this be the last year of my pilgrimage: I have travelled long enough on this side of the mountain.

In both instances his words may have been uttered in a moment of weariness or of exaltation, but they were not insincere. He was too intent upon his work to have many such moments. At the end of the 1690s when he was turning seventy he seemed to be carrying on almost as well as twenty years earlier. He was still active in his community, advising the schoolmaster who had just been discharged, reading Latin with the village boys and still studying by candlelight. He was occupied with another pamphlet, his *Book of Exceeding Joy*. Eleven months before his death he wrote to his son: 'My last and best journey will be to the up-hill city where I long to be.' In his last months he began to be overcome with drowsiness and to be more troubled with shortness of breath. He noted the symptoms of decay but without expressions of regret or self-pity. He had to be carried to his chapel in a chair, as Calvin had been. Once there he preached, as he believed, with his accustomed vigour. A month before his death he served the Lord's Supper, but had to call upon Jonathan Priestley for help. At home he sought the Lord constantly, as always, and seemed to have no fear of death. The final entries in his diary continue until within five days of his end and show increasing weakness and weariness. But none of the entries for the last months of his life give any hint of the struggles, of the heights and depths of his earlier life. He had attained to that quietness of spirit that was the proper accompaniment of his faith.

INDEX

INDEX

INDEX

Date Due
